distraction

a true story

To Gerry
From Satrece
May good spirit
live on!!

Satrece

PAGE PUBLISHING, INC.
New York, NY

First originally published by Page Publishing, Inc. 2017

ISBN 978-1-64027-171-5 (Paperback)
ISBN 978-1-64027-172-2 (Digital)

Printed in the United States of America

Success

Ralph Waldo Emerson

To laugh often and much;
To win the respect of intelligent people
and the affection of children;
To earn the appreciation of honest critics
and endure the betrayal of false friends;
To appreciate beauty, to find the best in others;
To leave the world a bit better, whether by a healthy child,
a garden patch or a redeemed social condition;
To know even one life has breathed easier
because you have lived.
This is to have succeeded.

distraction is dedicated to my four girlfriends in the United States, my source of reason and strength amid times of uncertainty while I lived in Bali and Java, and while I cruised the high seas. Tina Strarup, Karen Perdue, Mimi Osbourne and Kym Rodgers, thank you from the bottom of my heart for always being there. When I needed a friend, a place to stay, advice or just laughter, you made yourselves available and worried for me and my well-being. For two decades, you all have been the better friend to me than I to you. I am eternally grateful. Terima Kasih!

Contents

Acknowledgments

I would like to extend a warm thank you from the depths of my soul to my best friend for helping me through this project and for the unending support in every aspect and in every way. Thank you for the countless edits and the sustaining enthusiasm. You don't want to be mentioned here by name, but I doubt this book would exist without you. You are my North Star and my guiding compass.

I would also like to thank Carla Picard, the second person to read my book and offer suggestions, for her support until I got my groove. She gave me courage to push forward. Also Juliet Dunn of Retrospect Photography, based in Dubai, who did an absolutely fabulous job on the photographs for the logo, book cover, and website and Sharon Drugan who helped with my hair and makeup for the photos. Sanaulla of Oak Land Agriculture and Landscaping

made it possible to have tropical plants for my photo shoot in the desert heat of Dubai.

I don't want to forget Paul Sparks. Thank you for the outstanding creative work you did on the website, book cover, and logo. My gratitude to all for such whole-hearted support.

1

DFW Airport, Dallas, TX

pril 16, 2008. As Kym and I pull up to Departures at Dallas/Fort Worth Airport, I struggle with three huge and overweight pieces of luggage. It takes all my strength and leverage to get each out of the trunk of her Mercedes.

Kym is talking on her cell phone to a mega-customer who phoned her unexpectedly with a deal-buster problem. Kym is my good friend—we are both independent, strong, and successful women who take our business and responsibilities seriously. We also have big hearts and like helping others.

Kym has been on the call for nearly two hours, having conferenced in her technical people and her upper management in hopes of finding a resolution.

She volunteered to deliver me to the airport for my long international journey home to the remote village in which I live, thinking she had an open schedule. Instead of having me calling a taxi, she insists on multitasking by making her business call and driving me to DFW.

Her generous hospitality allowed me to use her home for my base as I travelled around the country meeting with my customers while culminating my business at the International Home Furnishings Center Market in High Point, North Carolina. Kym and I had been discussing how much I might owe her for the amenities that I consumed while staying at her home when her business call commenced.

Kym looks at me helplessly as I struggle to unload the luggage from her trunk. She places her call on mute, and we hug and say our good-byes until next time, whenever that might be. She is quickly back in her car again and on her way, so she can fully focus her attention on the customer and call.

This isn't like Asia, no porter is running to my rescue; I see the system here. I must deliver the luggage right to curbside check-in. I plead for help, and finally, a gentleman comes, so I promise him a considerable tip. The same procedure is happening that I

distraction

am so familiar with, as the porter explains, "All your luggage is *very* overweight, so I can't check you in here. I'll carry your luggage inside to the counter, and you will have to pay a rather large sum to get this luggage on." *Yeah, yeah, yeah,* I think *I know the program, I'll just pay it.*

As the porter and I are making our way to the counter, I reach into my purse to get my wallet so that I can pay his tip. *No wallet? Wait a minute, it has to be here; where is it?* As I continue to dig in my purse, it becomes clear; there is *no* wallet to be found. Dread begins to set in. "My wallet isn't in my purse; I can't imagine what has happened to it," I declare to the porter. He can tell by the look on my face that I'm in trouble. As we approach the counter and I have no money to pay him, I give him a look of exasperation while shrugging my shoulders and apologizing. He gives me a swoosh of his hand and exhales a miffed breath as he walks off. He knows my intentions are good, but I am presently helpless.

The lady at the counter tells me how overweight my luggage is and how much the airline is going to charge me for it. I stare at her with big eyes that say, "Houston, I've got a problem!" It hits me fiercely that my wallet is still sitting on Kym's kitchen counter

where I left it. I was planning to write her a generous check when she hung up from her phone call to
ensure I hadn't abused any privileges while staying
at her home. Instead, her conference call continued,
meaning we never officially finished our conversation, and I completely forgot to pick up my wallet
once we left for the airport. I explain the situation to
the lady who really isn't interested in my problems.
I try to call Kym who, of course, doesn't answer;
she's probably still tied up with her conference call.
Then I deduce that at this time of day, it would take
her nearly an hour to get home and another hour to
get back to the airport. That isn't enough time anyway. *What to do? What to do?* I try calling some of her
friends who live closer to the airport to ask for help
and assistance. No answers, none of them.

The lady at the counter is watching my desperation grow, and then I plead for her assistance in ideas
for alternatives. She at last concludes that I'm a gold
member of the airline, so that gives me an additional
baggage allowance, and I'm an international traveler,
so that's more of an allowance as well, and maybe,
if I rearrange my luggage and carry some things on,
that could get me close to the limits, and she could
help me a little.

I have my two suitcases and one duffel bag open and spread out across the airport floor, rearranging their contents and deciding what I can stuff into my carry-on computer bag and what else I may carry on. After immense effort, I now have two bags close enough to the limit that the lady accepts them. The last bag is still nearly twenty pounds overweight. If I'm going to get on this flight, it's going to mean I'll suffer severe consequences. I shuffle through the duffel bag that carries my personal shopping; I take a large bottle of both my luxurious, extra-hydrating shampoo and conditioner, walk to the closest trash can and toss them in, making sure that it makes a loud *clunk!* Surely, the lady has to be impressed with this move and will take pity on me.

Nooope, no pity, not even one ounce. She shakes her head from side to side knowing as I did that it was worth only about seven or eight pounds at most. I study my supply duffel bag again, achingly deciding what treasures I would surrender that would make a significant weight difference. I pull out the large bottle of Grey Goose L'Orange Vodka, the king-size 1.75 liters, walk back to the trash can and hold it over the opening. I wait to hear her say, "No, it's not necessary!" But there is only silence!

Knowing I have no choice, I release my fingers and let the vodka fall hard to the bottom, generating an even louder *clunk!* An audience has now gathered and is watching this spectacle.

As I walk back to the counter, the lady waves at me to put the duffel bag up on the conveyor belt. It worked! I'm on the flight! After my display of desperation—coupled with the bravery and sacrifices I make—the lady doesn't even bother to weigh the bag for my final check-in.

Meanwhile, I vaguely notice an attractive man passing through my peripheral vision, a man named Ron, a successful and suave international businessman. I'll learn later that he is good at what he does and loves his job. In fact, Ron is good at *everything* he does, and he does it all: tennis, golf, skiing, basketball, baseball, Harley riding, billiards, foosball, hunting and fishing and even socializing. He's either the life of the party, or he's the sophisticated gentleman quietly sitting in the corner and evaluating everyone. He's a fearless worldwide traveler with great street smarts, yet he is kind and compassionate. He is known for his courtly elegance and is well-respected for his savvy acumen. Most of his social life is with his colleagues or customers. His work is his life.

Ron First Notices Satrece

"Holy shit!" he says to a colleague, Bob, with whom he's talking on a cellphone, updating him on his recent meeting. "You cannot believe the beautiful, gorgeous woman I'm looking at! I need to figure out a way to meet her."

"Really, buddy? Where are you?" Bob asks.

Ron answers, "DFW airport. I finished my meetings early but catching an earlier flight back to Houston isn't an option."

Bob is one of his closest buddies at the office; they get each other. He looks to Ron as a mentor of sorts, but they often have engaging talks about life in general. Bob's a great guy; the salt of the earth, honest, sincere, and ethical. He'd do anything for Ron, and he knows Ron has his back covered. They've had great times together; some off-the-charts fun. They call each other "brotha from a different motha."

"Tell me what she looks like."

"She's *hot!* I really mean it! To describe her, I have to say she's outrageously beautiful! She appears elegant and sumptuous. She's really, really *beautiful!* Just *stunning!*"

"Are you really going to talk to her? What are you going to say?"

"If she would ever get off of her cell phone, I'll talk to her. I don't know yet."

"You've got to make your first impression count, let's precall this."

"How about, it's great to see a woman take such good care of herself."

"Oh man, that entire approach *and* words are cheesy! You can't say that; she'll blow you off even before you get started. You have to do better than that. That's ridiculous; how about saying something like: 'You are just so beautiful I had to come over and introduce myself'…?"

"No, I need more than that; she's too beautiful for a line like that. That's just not me; I'll figure it out, and whatever I say will just come out and usually is the right thing, I always do well when put on the spot," Ron says assuredly.

Hanging up from Bob, he sees "the woman" is still on her cell phone. He cannot help but be curious that she is dressed completely in khaki. Her designer blouse is tailored to highlight her curves. To look at her is bewitching. He is immediately drawn to her large, voluptuous breasts, baring just enough cleav-

age to be intriguing and sexy. She is tall with beautiful long legs and a perfectly shaped round ass! He can see that she is deeply tanned. Her long, thick brown hair is cascading over her shoulders. Her makeup is perfect, flawless, though she has it slightly understated, looking naturally beautiful. Ron is truly drawn to all of her—from her enticing full lips, which he cannot stop staring at, all the way down to her toes connected to the cutest little feet.

Normally, he'd have gone straight to the Continental President's Lounge, but for some unexplainable reason, today he went directly to the gate. It must be his lucky day.

Besides her, there are only two other people at the gate, both men, and both are trying to get her attention. "Get the hell away from her!" Ron thinks. He sees her as *his*! Pondering "the first line," he decides to pace the airport.

Satrece First Takes Notice of Ron

I am completely absorbed in the conversation on my cellphone, trying to determine how to handle my new dilemma, when something in my peripheral vision catches my attention again. I look up to see that man

strolling by, and now *he* has my full attention. I can't help but think, *wow*, he's had a good day. Look at that smile on his face and how confident he looks. He *exudes* success. I can't help but to simply admire him; it's not too often you see a man like this. He's a man with commanding presence, and stands well over six feet with large, broad shoulders. He walks like a man with purpose. And look at his smile; it is absolutely dazzling. I wonder what it is that makes him smile like that. Ahh, and now I see he's just glanced my way. He's a man who knows what he wants and most likely gets it, too. I bet under that sports jacket, he's built. His type wields power. I am certain he's married; at least there is one lucky lady in the world. Wouldn't it be ironic as much as I travel if I were to meet the man of my dreams in an airport? "Man" and "dreams" are *not* two words that I typically would put in the same sentence. Snickering at myself, I turn my attention back to my phone call in progress.

After finishing the call, I look up and around the airport in search of him, curious if the second impression would rival the first, but he is nowhere to be found. Shortly thereafter, I see him walking to the gate area. He chooses a seat across from me, not too far; however, not too close either.

Ron Meets Satrece

She looks troubled; something has her attention. Ron wonders what the problem is; maybe he can help. Ahhhh, she hung up her phone, now what? How does he talk to her? He continues to contemplate his plan on how to get the courage to go up to this gorgeous creature and engage her in conversation. *She's got to be married, too lovely not to be, though she's not wearing a ring.*

Then before he can second-guess his courage, he's speaking. "It's great to see a woman take such good care of herself," comes blurting out of his mouth. *Not even an "excuse me," or "may I interrupt" or... or...or...what an idiot! Too late now.*

Satrece's First Impression

I am immediately offended; I tilt my head and study him with this absurd comment coming from what I'd guessed was an intelligent guy. I am not in the mood for this today. I look into his eyes, trying to figure out or understand why he led with this rather illogical line. I thought I was a pretty good judge of character, until right now. This man senses my mood; I'm not smiling nor am I exhibiting any signs of pleas-

antry. Then I reply, quite sternly, "Exactly, *what* do you mean by *that?*"

Ron's not used to being challenged, and he throws his head back for a full, deep, belly laugh.

I notice his dazzling smile again, and to my surprise, it actually causes me to smile too.

Ron looks directly back into my eyes matching my stare and decides to come up with something intelligent before he opens his mouth again. "Well, that didn't come out exactly like I wanted it to. Let me try this again. So, do you live in Dallas or Houston?"

"Neither."

Surprised by her answer, he smiles and asks, "Where are you traveling to?"

"A long way from here," I reply with a smug look on my face.

"Where?"

"Far away."

"How far?"

"A long way."

"How long?"

"To the other side of the world." *Doesn't this guy get it? I have no time for a man who lives in America, assuming that he does, no matter how fetching or handsome he may be.*

distraction

"Where on the other side of the world?" Ron asks as he realizes that I am toying with him now. He recognizes this is a carousel of exchanges that I am using to prevent him from entering into my world.

I see him laugh, his interest is piqued; he is up for the challenge. He decides to see how long I'm going to play this game, and he's going to rally back along with me. This further proves my assessment of him accurate.

"Home."

"Where's home?"

At this point, I hesitate, and at last I say, "I'm going home to Indonesia."

As his eyes pierce into mine, he scrutinizes me more closely, and I can see a thousand thoughts erupt through Ron's mind. I bet he is thinking, *Hmm... intriguing. Is she telling me the truth, or is she simply dismissing me? What would possess her to live in Indonesia?*

Ron asks, "Kamu bisa bicara Bahasa Indonesia?" (Can you speak the Indonesian language?) *Well, this gets my attention!*

Like having a noose around my neck, I'm jerked to attention. In response, my index finger innately wants to poke in my ear and clear it out. Now I ponder him, *Have I been living in Indonesia so*

long that I'm actually hearing "strangers" in Dallas, Texas, speaking Bahasa to me? Ahh, I get it, he's testing me. Bombarding him and speaking rapidly I say, "Pasti, saya bisa bicara Bahasa Indonesia, baik sekali. Tetapi, bagimana kamu belajar? Ahh, saya mengertti, kamu tinggal de Houston sekarang, kamu kerja di bisnis minyak dan sudah tinggal de Jakarta sebentar ..." (Sure, I can speak the Indonesian language, very well. But how did you learn? Ahh, I understand; you live in Houston now, you work in the oil and gas business, and you lived in Jakarta for a while ...)

He throws his hands up in the air and broadly smiling from ear to ear, he says, "Betul (correct). You win! Enough, you *can* speak Bahasa. So you really do live there?" Ron asks in amazement.

"Yes, of course. Why else would I have said so?"

"What do you do in Indonesia? What brings you to the States?" Ron inquires quizzically.

So he *was* originally testing me, but I see he didn't understand everything that I said quickly, so I astutely repeat in English to him what I'd said in Bahasa.

Impressed with my assessment, he says, "Yep, you got it. My scenario is simple to figure out, but I'm still not clear why you are there?"

I ignore his questions again and begin bantering with him. I lead the conversation a little more in Indonesian to see how well he can keep up. Now I am positively impressed with Ron! Also, I realize that I am much more attentive and motivated to converse; we eventually resume our conversation in English.

So he's succeeded in drawing me in. *Who would've thunk it,* I joke to myself, *meeting a "gent" speaking to me in fluent Bahasa in Dallas of all places. WOW!*

Finally, answering his previous questions, I add, "I own a furniture manufacturing company in Central Java. I've been here in the States meeting with my customers and have just finished exhibiting my new designs in the North Carolina Furniture Show. It's the largest furniture show in the world."

"Do you live there full-time, or do you commute back and forth?"

"I live there full-time…that would be a rather long commute, don't you think?"

"Central Java, huh…how long have you lived there?"

"About fifteen years now."

"Fifteen years …. Really? By the way, my name is Ron, what's yours?"

Satrece

"My name is Satrece. It's nice to meet you, Ron, you are quite the surprise. So what brings you to Dallas today?"

"I had a business meeting in the area today. Actually, it's odd that I'm here talking with you at DFW. I flew into Dallas Love Field early this morning, and it's strange that I couldn't get a flight out, so here I am at DFW chatting with you. But somehow, I think it's my lucky day."

"So, Ron, what do you do? Looks to me like you had a good day today."

Grinning, he says, "Yes, I did have a great day. Ahhhh…what I do is boring. I'd rather talk about you some more. I noticed earlier that you seemed troubled."

"Yes, as a matter of fact, I am."

Ron asks, "Is there anything I can do to help? What's troubling you?"

"It's complicated, but I have it figured out. The long and short of it, I left my wallet on the counter of my girlfriend's house where I was visiting. I'm trying to determine if I can travel to the other side of the world without one penny to my name. I'm in Business First all the way so that helps, and when I get to Bali, they know me well enough at the Villa

distraction

that I can put the taxi charge on my room bill. I'll hit the bank immediately Monday morning after I arrive."

"Well, we can go to the ATM right now, and I'll get you one thousand dollars!"

Astonishment and laughter take me by surprise. "Rreally? One thousand dollars? Wouldn't one hundred or two be more reasonable to offer up?"

"No, I'm serious," Ron says with resolve.

"I was able to contact my brother who lives in Houston, and he'll meet me at the airport with some money. Besides, he's coming to Indonesia in a few weeks to stay with me for a while. He can bring my wallet, and I'll settle up with him then."

Why does he keep staring at my feet and smiling? What's that all about?

"Are you sure? This is an easy one," Ron says.

I notice many more people gathering at the gate, and it's getting lively and noisy. However, I swear he's speaking more and more softly to boot. As I struggle to hear what he's saying, I'm getting extremely frustrated. Why is he speaking to me in such a soft tone, barely above a whisper? Is it worth my time and effort to continue this conversation? Decision time, do I simply end this now? He must know what he's

doing; I won't allow him or anything else to irritate me. But I finally meet a person who is stimulating and enticing, and I'm enjoying the conversation with him. And that *splendid* smile! Amazed at myself, and standing up without even contemplating it, I ask, "Do you mind if I move closer, so I can hear you?" I select a seat next to him, leaving one empty seat in-between.

"Certainly. Please!" Ron smiles smugly, learning later that his strategy worked.

Sitting in our own little world, captivated by each other and the conversation, no longer noticing the commotion around us, an announcement is made, "Continental Flight #614 to Houston is delayed approximately fifty minutes." We look at each other, smile and shrug with indifference, then continue conversing like we were long-lost friends with a flowing, familiar connection.

The time flies by when our flight to Houston is called.

"Well, Satrece, I have to be on this flight, and it seems that I've lost my boarding pass. Are you certain I can't help you with some cash?"

"No, thank you. I'll be fine."

"It's been a real pleasure meeting you, Satrece."
This lady has rattled his world. Ron is known as the
person who can fluently converse with leaders of
countries and the management of Fortune 500 companies. *He WILL find her again. He knows her first name
and the village she lives in …. Jepara, Jepara, Jepara. He can't
forget where she lives, that's all he needs. Ron knows Indonesia
well, and he is certain that she is the only tall, slender hot-
lookin' Western white woman in the village. Everybody will
know her if he can get to the village and ask for Satrece. You
know, the tall pretty woman from Texas. He will find her.*

After receiving his new boarding pass, he
immediately looks into the crowd of people. She is
nowhere to be found. Damn!

Sitting in row 1, aisle seat, I watch what seems
to be the majority of the passengers board. I look
around and see that the first-class cabin is full with
the exception of one seat. I think it's odd that I hav-
en't seen "him" board the flight. He seemed to be a
first-class type of guy. Is he really on this flight, or
was he simply sitting at the gate to meet me?

Being disappointed that he lost her, Ron enters
the Boeing 737. *What? There she is!* "She" is sitting in

first-class, row 1, *next* to *him*! Following his normal routine, Ron begins taking his laptop and iPod from his bag in the overhead; he can't help but look at her loveliness and makes a quick decision: this stuff isn't really important right now. Ron puts everything back, and he figures that the whole world can wait. He wants every minute he can steal with this woman. Will he ever see her again after this flight?

I look up just then, and there he stands!

The flight attendant asks me what I want to drink, and I quip, "Champagne, please. This is my first leg of many to go."

I am met with the reply of, "Sorry, ma'am, we no longer serve champagne on domestic flights."

I roll my eyes and comment, "What's this country coming to? White wine will do. Thank you."

"I'll have what she's having and keep them coming," Ron says with a broad smile.

He continues to study me while we engage and consume some wine together. He finally gets the nerve to ask the silly question he had been waiting to ask, "Are your feet a perfect size 7½?"

"Yes, they are, as a matter of fact. I noticed you staring at my feet earlier. What's that about?" I chide.

Ron simply shrugs and smiles with a delighted look upon his face. I learn quickly how uniquely perceptive and expressive this man is; he has already commented on my "alluring makeup," my cute feet, and how my toe polish matches the jewels on my heeled sandals.

The one-hour flight to Houston had to be the quickest hour of our lives. During the short flight, we discussed in more detail my business and how I ended up in Indonesia. We laughed together, and the fascination with each other continued while we touched down. Departing the flight and not ready to say good-bye, Ron offers to escort me to where I agreed to meet my brother. I spot my brother and Ron and I say good-bye.

What's curious is the fact that Ron only knows her first name and the village where she lives. Ron continues to ask himself, *will I be able to find her?*

I'm relieved to meet my brother as planned, and now I have the cash to get home. I've just enough time to make my connecting flight. Elated to be going home, walking through the airport, I'm singing in my head, "Do wah-diddy, diddy-dum, diddy-do."

Having sensed something unusual, I stop abruptly and scan what's around me. Twenty feet in

front of me stands Ron at a Continental podium, his head resting on his hand and his eyes piercing me with a very pensive stare. Astonished, I ask, "What are you doing here?"

"I need to make certain you'll be okay and don't need any money. My offer still stands," he says.

With the radiance he had seen earlier and an enamored smile, Satrece replies, "I wasn't sure if guardian angels still existed."

Ecstatic to see her warm response and anxious to steal every moment that he could with her, Ron asks, "Satrece, can I walk with you, at least to security?"

"I would be honored," as I extend my arm for him to escort me as far as security allows.

What I didn't know in those brief moments after saying good-bye the second time, Ron had put his foot on the electric door to exit the airport terminal, the door opened, and he stepped outside. Stopping and considering, he thought, "*If this is what I think it can be, I'd better go back inside the airport and find her.*" Ron did just that.

As we depart from each other for the third time that day, I hand Ron my business card and give him a warm hug, pausing a moment with a small kiss on his

distraction

left cheek while softly saying and inviting, "If you are ever in my part of the world, look me up."

Ron, besieged with emotion, looks deeply into my eyes and says, "You can count on it, I promise." He then reaches into his bag, retrieves a business card and places it in my hand.

As he watches her walk away, he sees her take one last glance back at him.

2

The Flight Home
to Indonesia

As my flight departs Bradley International Airport, the lights of Los Angeles lay beneath me, one step of many in getting home. I have been in the States for a month, meeting my customers, engaging in trade shows, taking care of business. Additionally, I took time to shop for important necessities like skin care, vitamins, etc., all of the things best purchased stateside. Hmmm, thoughts of Ron keep interrupting my other "important" thoughts. Why had fate brought us together? Is that what it was…fate? I am a woman of Southeast Asia. Southeast Asia is my home; I love it there. With me being a woman of Asia and he a

man of Texas, what could come of this? Absolutely nothing, that's what. But we met three times in the same day. Well, enough of thinking about that.

Just to get home, I have three airlines, five airplanes, and several days of travel. I have Dallas to Houston, Houston to LA behind me, just Taipei to go and onward to Bali, eventually getting home to Jepara, Java. In this thirteen-hour leg of this forty-two-hour journey in the tranquility of the late night, I always find myself getting sentimental and emotional about my life, my home. It's my first bit of quiet time since I landed in the States a month ago. How do people live like this, not having quiet time and silence in their lives?

I am *so* happy to be going home, going to my home in Southeast Asia. It is a place of extremes. It is a place of sweltering heat and unending tirades of rain that cause flash floods and instant mudslides. It can rain so hard that one would think it's not possible to rain any harder, but it does. Southeast Asia holds its own mystique, unique from any other place in the world. It's fascinating; it's exotic. It's a world of contradictions. It possesses an immense diversity of land, people, and cultures. It is complicated, yet simple. It is hard, yet soft. The water is not potable.

I have seen the strongest man brought to his knees by a mere sip. But the smells, the sights, the sounds make the same man smile again. I love it because it IS the tropics; "different latitudes bring different attitudes," no matter the hemisphere. Its rainforests are abundant with the tropical flora marking the entire region. I love its vast seas and the ocean trade winds; one is never too far from the coast here. I love the heat; I hate the heat. I love how the rain makes everything so lush; I hate the monsoons. I can hate the people because they are so simple, but again, I love them because they are so simple. I love banana trees and coconut trees, how every bit of them help sustain life. As food, they are filled with protein and many important nutrients. One minute, a banana leaf shades the sun, and soon, it will be the only umbrella around. This place I call home, it's an amazing, amazing place.

It's incredible that I call *Jepara* my home. Many people are satisfied to call Dallas, Los Angeles or London, Paris or Tokyo home. But no, not I. I chose a small, remote village in Indonesia, in Central Java on the northern coast to be exact. It was a small place at the time that I moved there amid Islamic peasants struggling through daily life, where fishing had

been the main industry. Most of the time, the people were delighted to have a handful of rice for the day, considered it lucky if were mixed with a few bites of chicken or egg and red chilies or cabe as they're called in Bahasa. The entire area is thick with lush forest and flora—the jungle, as I call it. I live in The Jungle. It's still hard even for me to believe, and more so that I have lived here since age twenty-nine. Who would have known that my destiny in life would be more than a decade and a half in the jungle and still counting? Until now, my life is living among, learning from, helping and assisting, educating and loving; yes, *loving*, some of the poorest people in the world. The average person here has more heart and more soul than anyone I could have imagined. A large percentage of these people live below the poverty line. It's a world that many Westerners can't fathom, but it is MY life. It seems to be my destiny. From my experience, few from the Western world understand or can comprehend this life, my life. Now I realize, for some unknown reason, I have exiled myself into this jungle.

It *was* a jungle, not so much now. It found an industry, it grew, it blossomed, and it was known as the little-kept secret; however, it's still *very* rural.

People have since flocked here for jobs, but I fear this era is coming to an end. I find myself filled with emotions and various contradictory thoughts. I have given this place my heart, my soul, my prayers, all my strength, my might, my determination, and my love, though *true love has been the only thing that has managed to escape me.* The hard way of life I have chosen makes me a stronger person, a better person. I have learned patience, I have learned humility and compassion, I have learned to laugh when there is nothing to make me laugh, and I have learned to live with so little. I'm now focused on what is important in life. No more unnecessary and unimportant details, no more *stuff*, and no more *lists*. I know what it is that I seek in life today. How many can say that? It's more important than ever *HERE*, in this poor place, to pass it forward, even if it is as small as a kind word, a simple deed or just a smile. I now see the big picture; you give what you can with love, and the universe gives back to you. *Now*, I live in abundance. Friends in America think of me as insane, fifteen years in the jungle, in isolation. My factory employs 493 people. It supports 493 families inside the factory; and outside, it assists and supports hundreds and hundreds more. I find myself an important contributor to the local

economy, funding the orphanage, the elderly home, providing university and trade school scholarships, caring for the ill and less fortunate and other worthy causes. Here, the everyday way of life depends on me for so much. Most of my staff has been with me ten-to-thirteen years. They call me family, and I now refer to them as mine. It is a beautiful and lovely symbiotic relationship.

What is the next step the Big Man upstairs has planned for me? Going home again, I feel as I always do: immense happiness. My soul is in Asia. Actually, I simply don't belong in America anymore. Am I to live the rest of my life in the jungle? I have already started building my dream villa in the rice paddies of Tegalalang, north of Ubud in Bali. It is essentially a five-room boutique villa terraced on what used to be rice paddies; it will be an awesome life there, but a life all alone? And I met this most interesting man in the airport.

I yearn to travel to every far corner of this world. My soul has wings as I fly home and onward over these clouds. God made this gigantic world with many countries and cultures for a reason; it's a large playground for us all to attain wisdom, learn the balance of life and a richer sense of purpose. I have

searched for wisdom to unlock the perfection, which can be hidden by our personalities, revealing the glowing intelligence of our soul. As stated, "Ask and it shall be given; seek and you shall find; knock and the door shall be opened." The stars have entered my soul, and the awakening process has long been engaged.

I now get what life is about. There's a bit of God in every country, in every place, in every culture, and in every religion. There is even a little bit of God in each one of us. No one person or country or race or place or creed is perfect. If we each only draw from the good that's everywhere and learn to expel the bad, we can live a life of harmony and have an attitude of gratitude.

A man from Texas? Reeeally? Gjeeshk!

3

Ron after Departing from Satrece

*R*on strolls through the door of his luxury apartment in Houston, Texas, which is elaborately decorated. Having earned the status of Platinum member on several airlines, he wasn't home too often, so this type of accommodation had more than met his needs. The first thing he does is unpack his laptop and boot up. Having been consumed with thoughts of Satrece while driving home, he goes straight to her website to learn all that he can about her. He is instantly taken aback; an impressive website of all black and gold colors, regally done, dances across the screen with intricate, ornamental furniture designs that are extraordinary.

From reading, he learns that she *does* own her own business, has showrooms across the nation, and is well-established having been there as long as she said she was. "There, in the jungle? Stunningly beautiful and SUCCESSFUL, TOO?!" He thinks.

Ron, himself being a lover and collector of fine things, puts furniture at the top of his list. His apartment is decorated with art from well-known artists, including exquisite sculptures and lamps, and furniture made of many exotic woods. As he explored the website wanting to learn every detail possible about Satrece, he is "blocked" for not having a proper user ID and password. "How frustrating," he thinks to himself. "The most beautiful woman I have ever met, I want to know more, I need to know more, the information is at my fingertips, but I can't get to it! Damn it! Well, hell, she really isn't just a façade," he says out loud with fascination and relief.

As he begins to mechanically unpack his "Hartman," Ron can remember every detail of her. He first remembers Satrece's large, voluptuous breasts baring just enough to be sexy. He remembers her to be elegant in all aspects. She has the most intriguing, distinguishing mole—beauty mark—on her left cheek that reminds him of Cindy Crawford.

He will never forget those very looooong legs and perfectly rounded ass! With her heels, she stands over six feet tall, so he guesses that she is about five feet ten inches. She has a deeply tanned, slender body with big, thick, and long Texas brunette hair cascading over her shoulders. Ron remembers her impeccable makeup. He cannot forget those full lips, which made him want to kiss her right then and there. He truly wants to be with her. She's completely on his mind; yes, he is smitten! She was wearing bronze-colored heeled sandals decorated with rose-colored jewels; her toe polish matched the jewels. There is not one fault about her that he can remember. Ron walks back to the laptop, scours it again, wanting even more information if he can get at it, he reads:

"The exquisite collection emphasizes upscale and sophisticated designs. It includes fluted columns and arches, crowns and acanthus leaves. It is handcrafted by skilled artisans from exotic woods and veneers including mahogany wood. It includes delicate and intricate hand-carved, detailed works of refinement and elegance. From the wonderful hospitality of the dining room to the cozy, elegant ambiance of the den, original French, Italian and English furniture have inspired the appearances of our reproductions …"

So she is smart and accomplished. How *sexy* is *that*?! Ron knows her part of the world well. He's not been to Jepara, but he knows enough to know how to get there. That means she has more balls than most men he knows in the oil and gas industry. Along with her other attributes, she is obviously well-versed in the Bahasa Indonesian language too. There is still something more about her that fascinates him, but he just can't put his finger on it. Once he broke that barrier around her, there was warmth and kindness, but also a determined and daring spunk. He has met his match, he realizes. He has totally met his match.

As his arms wrap around her warm and sleek body, he wants every inch of her close to him. Her kisses are surrendering to him, but he wants ALL of her to surrender to him. Her perfume is intoxicating. He looks at her and thinks…*outrageous*! He realizes that she is his poster woman of sexy! As he caresses her breasts and lightly kisses her full lips, their tongues dance. His arm is wrapped around her waist, and he is holding her closely. She has her legs wrapped around his, and he can feel her desire building. Her thick, full hair is unbelievable. He looks into her piercing eyes that tell him she is thirsting for their passion. Her skin is just so soft and smooth; it feels

lovely. He wants to wake up with her, with their bodies entwined as they are now. He wants, he wants... *BUZZ! BUZZ! BUZZ!* "That damned alarm!" as he rolls out of bed, jolted and wrenched with frustration to start his day.

Ron walks into his office early the next morning, throws the Hartman bag he always totes onto his desk and walks promptly into Bob's office. "Bob, you aren't going to believe the beautiful woman I just met."

Bob perks up behind his desk and says, "What woman?"

"The woman at the airport yesterday."

"You mean the woman that we did a precall on? Tell me more."

"Yes, that one. Not only is she beautiful and has one hell of a sexy body, she is intelligent and successful, interesting, adventurous, has balls of steel, and I have the feeling she is as pretty on the inside as she is on the outside."

"Umm, so you actually met her yesterday? And went on a date last night?" Bob asked looking confused.

"No. We only spoke in the airport; she was in transit."

Bewildered, Bob asked, "And you know all of this, how?"

"Well, we spent three hours together yesterday. It was amazing. Once I got home, I checked out her website, and I really know well the part of the world where she lives."

"So your opening line worked then, what did you say?" Bob continues to smile and says, "Tell me more!" Now, he's anxious to hear every detail.

"The one we discussed with a little more smooth delivery," Ron slightly misleads.

"You're kidding me. I told you it was cheesy! She liked it? It worked?" Bob asked with complete interest but still confused.

Ron laughs. "No, she didn't like it. She actually challenged me on it. But what can I say, buddy? Mission accomplished."

Ron fills Bob in on all that happened, what he learned about this woman, where she lives, as much of her life that he knew and, of course, Ron's assumptions.

"RD, I am happy for you, but I don't understand. You said she lives on the other side of the world full-time and has NO intentions of coming back to the States or even to Texas? So why are you so excited?"

"Fair enough question," as Ron pauses and ponders it himself. "I'm not sure, but I have to get to know her better and see if she is everything that I think she is. Once you find what could be your true love, you should never let her go."

Ron feels like he has been looking for something or somebody his whole life. The moment he saw Satrece, he knew what that something or somebody was. It was the piece he still needed to make his life complete. Once he met her, she seemed to be everything he had ever dreamed of, and more. He had to know if this was truly the case—he *needed* to know. If she is as she seems, he'll figure out what's next when that time comes. And IF she's married, he will then decide how he handles that too.

What Ron doesn't realize is that as much as he wants love in his life, he had created a life without love. Would love now fit into his hectic work-related social calendar and global lifestyle? This is the life that he now loves. And if Satrece is all that he is looking for, has she built the life she loves? Have they each already built their perfect lives? Perfect lives built for each to live completely alone?

"I know you are good in what you do, Ron, known for pulling a rabbit out of the hat when nec-

essary and a master when it comes to strategy, but buddy, I think you're in over your head on this one."

Laughing out loud, "Maybe so, Bob, but I think she could be *the one*. I guess tonight I'll give our buddies in Singapore a call and see what's happening in Asia Pacific. It's been a while since I've been there, but I hear there are some big things going on, and I'm pretty certain they could use my help."

Bob just shakes his head as Ron strolls out of his office, thinking his poor friend has lost his mind, and over a woman!

4

Satrece Landing in Bali

*L*anding in Bali, I am assaulted by 100 percent humidity. It was the first outdoor fresh air that I experienced in more than forty hours. The afternoon sun is bright and hard on my jet-lagged eyes. Oh, but the smells of Bali, the dupa (incense), hovering in the air, the many food carts clanking close by, the fragrant flowers everywhere, the sounds of gamelan music always in the background wherever you go, and the smoldering heat. I make my way to Villa Heliconia, which is just blocks away from the beach and the Indian Ocean, a small, private villa where I often stay while in Bali. The desk clerk, Made', is awaiting my arrival. Made' gives me a warm smile and says, "Ah, Ibu Satrece,

Satrece

selamat datang. Apa kabar?" (Ah, Ms. Satrece, welcome. How are you doing?)

I chime back, "Baik sekali, terima kasih." (I'm doing well, thank you.)

Made' asks, "Senang ke bertamu kamu lagi, berapa lama disini?" (I'm pleased to see you again, and how long will you be here?)

After all the normal greetings are said in the beautiful singsong tempo always spoken by the Balinese, I explain that I will be staying only for a few days, and how happy I am to be back. I enter my villa, unpack a few things and quickly organize myself. I peel the garments off that I've worn while traveling the past two days and think to myself, aaahhh, it's so nice to get out of these clothes; at last to stretch, to walk, to move and to breathe fresh air. My private blue mosaic pool is enticing. Totally naked, I walk to it, dive in and swim the length of the pool underwater. I come up for air, swim several more laps, do some stretches and frolic in the cool water. Eventually, I hop onto the side of the pool and work my way to the teak lounger. Lying back, I enjoy the welcome drink made from fresh mango; how I love this, basking in the sun as it shines down warmly on my naked body. A deep, dark tan is

a priority to me. The water glistens as it rolls off my skin; the soft breeze caresses my breasts. Birds chirp and sing while the sweet fragrance of flowers floats through the air and palm trees sway rhythmically to the ocean breeze. Breathing in deep breaths of the fresh air with my body soaking in the rays of the sun, I finally begin to clear my mind. Life doesn't get any better than this for me. Why would anybody want to live anywhere else?

The next morning, I awake with the roosters; after all, I am adjusting to a thirteen-hour time difference. Provisions are necessary before I depart Bali for home. I have particular sources and wholesalers for the numerous things needed to sustain life including food, supplies, tools for the factory, and all things to make life and work comfortable. Because I live so remotely and Bali is my best source for fresh food, I treat myself to tenderloins, veal, salmon, scallops, lamb chops, cheeses, teas, fresh coffee, and whatever else I can find. The meats and fish are all portioned and packaged on dry ice for the long trip home. I will also purchase fresh vegetables for the first week. I will buy wine and spirits if I can find them, none of which are available in my neck of the woods.

Satrece

My Bali driver, Nyoman, picks me up at 9:00 a.m.; things start slowly in Bali, unlike Java. The bank will be our first stop. If all goes well, I will be fortunate to return to the villa by six or seven tonight. Boy, the traffic has gotten so bad in Seminyak through the years. I choose to let Nyoman battle the traffic, the habitual loud horn honking amid the million scooters ten lanes thick during the day, while I sit back and allow my brain to adjust to driving on the left side of the road. Soon, I will be shifting gears with my left hand; I need the time to let my brain assimilate all of this again. Upon returning back to the villa late in the evening after a successful day, I unload and repack all the provisions and label them for the remaining leg of the trip home. I again strip off my clothes, frolic in the pool, and enjoy a few glasses of wine in the gardens. It is my last day of peace for the foreseeable future.

A long journey home lies ahead of me. The next morning, I fly into Yogyakarta, Java, where my longtime driver, Rifan, greets me. We then drive northward through the mountains and around the volcanoes. It is typically a five-to-seven-hour drive from Yogya to home, depending on traffic, rain, floods, and mudslides. However, I know that there will be

nothing normal about this trip home today. It will definitely be a challenging one, knowing the current civil unrest. Rifan departed Jepara a day early, as he was anxious to be in Yogya prior to my arrival due to the likely demonstrations he would meet along the way. This also allowed him to appraise the situation.

The financial crisis of 2007 that emerged in America hit Indonesia hard, fast, and unexpectedly. Prior to my trip to the U.S., the *Jakarta Post* reported that the Indonesian economy would largely escape the effects of a looming global economic downturn. During the thirty days I was away, the World Bank reported that 130 to 155 million people in Southeast Asia were driven into poverty by the soaring food and fuel prices. The World Bank is now reporting that this will bring the total of those living on less than U.S. $2 per day to over 1.5 billion. The stock markets all over Southeast Asia are plummeting, and the exchange rates are depreciating significantly. It is quickly becoming a worldwide crisis, and the world economies are spiraling downward, including my beloved Indonesia. Prices of everything are escalating out of control. While on my trip, I was on the phone from the States nearly every day with my staff

discussing the new challenges we are now facing at the factory and the villages.

The daily news continues to broadcast about the uprisings and demonstrations occurring around the world demanding subsidies from their governments. These are difficult times, and people are struggling everywhere; unemployment explodes, the wars in the Middle East are not easing, and oil has hit a record price of $140 a barrel. The entire country is starving, but authorities seem unconcerned, still believing that the strong growth, robust fiscal conditions and the steady inflow of investments will still prevail. A fiscal package is yet to be considered for increasing subsidies for food and fuel, which are both now out of reach for the people. They can no longer afford to buy daily necessities. Indonesia, being the largest Muslim country in the world, severed many ties with Western countries supporting the wars in Iraq, and it created a significant number of additional challenges throughout the country. In short, the rupiah, the Indonesian currency, plummeted, so now the country's people cannot afford food, fuel or transportation, and they're enraged. The entire country is in disarray. The local governments are ordering "the people" to demonstrate against their employers and

distraction

big government. This is done in hopes that assistance will come to "the little people" of Java.

There will be tens of thousands of people in and on the roads during our journey home. Rifan says it took ten hours the previous day for him to make the trip, and I should expect nothing less than a flood of demonstrations. Java is in the top ten of the most densely populated places in the world, so the torrents of people demonstrating will present an extensive challenge. Our journey around the volcanoes, through the mountains and into the low lands is challenging as we work our way through the masses of humanity. It devours my heart seeing the distressed faces of the people on the roads. I can't help but think of the disparity here: my four-wheel-drive SUV is packed full of my shopping and supplies from America and Bali, yet the native Indonesians simply want to know that they will have a meal tomorrow. It is late that night when I arrive home, but I know that sleep will evade me. I worry about these indigenous people that I share a country with, and that I feel so strongly for. I honestly love them, and now I worry about how badly this economic crisis will affect them.

I go into the factory early the next morning, already aware that everyone is ordered by the local officials to demonstrate, and that my employees are anticipating my arrival. I ride into the factory with Rifan. In times of unrest, I never drive alone but always have the extra protection and knowledge of a local. I see *all* the workers of my factory sitting and hanging near the office door. All *seems* peaceful, yet no one is working.

I get out, greet them with a big smile, "Selamat pagi." (Good morning.)

The response comes back sung like a lullaby, "Selamat pagi, Ms. Satrece. Apa Kabar? Rindu kau, senang sudah kembali." (Good morning, Ms. Satrece. How are you? We missed you, we're very pleased for your return.)

I'm met with a consortium of managers and supervisors who follow me into the offices. After all the initial greetings and small talk, an appointed supervisor says to me in Indonesian, "You know that we should be demonstrating right now because of the changes that have occurred while you were away. We the villagers are not making enough wages to buy food or daily items that are needed. We can't afford to buy fuel either nor pay for transportation to get to

work. Our local governments insist for us to demonstrate until you, our employers, raise our wages to meet our needs. But, however, we know, and we have trust in you, Ms. Satrece, you will do the right thing for us…Correct?"

Without hesitation, I say, "Of course, the staff is already working on the numbers, so we know how much is needed to get you back where you were before the economy crashed. We hope to have it in your wages at the end of this week. I see and understand what you're going through. I understand the 'basic nine' items you need to sustain your daily life. If any additional assistance is needed, I will do anything in my power to help you and your families as I did in the 1997 crisis." This is my promise to them, and I receive big, warm smiles and handshakes, many "terima kasih's" (thank yous), as they have no worries; they know they can count on me. Back to work they go, harder than ever, and that is the extent of the demonstrations at my factory.

It isn't quite the same for many other factories in town; many other owners have their *own* challenges. Their businesses are in a downward spiral, and costs are spiraling up out of control. Many businesses will not survive. For these owners, com-

passion isn't at the top of their list right now. For those not compassionate to the cause, their production is stopped, factories are burned, and *their* lives descend into turmoil. It's the same for the rest of the country and the rest of Southeast Asia. I have saved and planned for these times, so hopefully, I am sufficiently prepared. I certainly have seen my share of unrest and have learned quickly from it. In turn, I'm shown and treated with respect, trust, and adoration during the height of strife and distress. In the weeks to come, the challenges are never-ending. One by one, the products and materials needed to manufacture my furniture become unavailable; one by one, we find a solution with our vendors. Mostly, they need large price increases to be able to produce their goods. How am I to sustain these higher costs when my customers are becoming aware that their sales are dropping? Well, *in god we trust.*

I am told that there is no fuel for the compressors and generators. Fuel is in such shortage that all "unnecessary" needs are denied, and only private vehicles are allowed to get fuel. In a sympathetic attempt to help the people, the local government begins to make foolish decisions. Businesses are denied fuel; only private citizens can buy fuel

for daily needs. It doesn't occur to these local decision makers that we, the businesses, need this fuel to operate and thus pay the people's wages so they have money to buy fuel. GJEESHK! It is suggested that we use my personal vehicle to get fuel, allowing it to be syphoned at the factory to run the machinery. I certainly don't have any better ideas at the moment, so back and forth it goes to get fuel, again and again. It is an unpredictable time requiring determination. My staff and I put out one fire after the other as the week goes by. I also know that this is just the beginning of many more weeks like this to come, possibly months. Finally, the week comes to an end; in Central Java, it is a six-day workweek. It seemed like this week had been the longest week ever.

Sunday, my first day off in Jepara since my return, is also my *only* day off. I start this morning like I do every morning at home. I leave my bedroom and go into the kitchen in the open pavilion. I grab for my beautiful fragrant and oily coffee beans, mixed from all regions of Indonesia, hand grind the beans and French press a lovely pot of coffee. My three cats come running to greet me; honestly, I should call them my psychotherapists or at least my shrinks. Living alone in isolation, it is my cats that I talk to; all

problems get discussed, funny stories get reported, and any essential bitching is disclosed. They listen particularly well when I just need to bare my soul. My trio always understands, they are accepting, and they are great listeners. There's Milo, a beautiful, large Himalayan male who I liberated from a life in a very small cage. He is as timid as they come and afraid of his own shadow. He is a skittish and frightened soul. Then there's Matsu, a one-eyed cat I retrieved from the factory that wouldn't have survived had I not brought him home and nursed him back to health. "Mata satu" means one-eyed in Bahasa; hence the play on his name, Matsu. He is a loyal and fat cat that knows he hit the mother lode of luck living here with me. And finally, Ms. Sascha; she is the chosen one. She is a registered blue and biscuit Persian that is wise, curious, witty, athletic, adventuresome, and sweet. I searched all of Bali and Java for her and her special companionship.

Being my first day off since returning, it's the one that always catches me by surprise: no domestic help, no one to talk to, no place to go, nothing to do. Just my cats and me. Reality hits: Back into isolation, and I wonder what it is that I like so much about the jungle and isolation. With coffee in hand, cats at my

heels, I head to my sofa in the pavilion that's facing my three-tiered twelve-foot waterfall. It is lushly
planted with lotus flowers, papyrus, frangipani trees,
bougainvillea, and other beautiful tropical flowers of
the area. Shiva sits in the middle of the bottom pond.
Shiva is one of the Hindu deities known as the Great
God or also regarded as the Supreme God. It is here
in my mystical gardens and waterfall that the wisdom
I seek always comes. I savor the accomplishments
of the week. All of these people and their families
depend on me, and I haven't let them down. Their
wages are increased approximately 35 percent for
now until we see where the price of things settle,
their jobs are secure, and other efforts needed will
be undertaken. They are ecstatic that I am home and
even happier that I exist. A dreadful week has passed,
and I am fulfilled and at peace.

On a typical Sunday, I seldom turn on my cell
phone, as there is no one to call nor anyone to talk
to. I decide to call some of my stateside girlfriends
as I promised I would, to let them know I've arrived
safely, and that all is well. It's after 10 a.m. my time,
which makes it nearly midnight Saturday night for
most of them. Surprise, surprise, no one answers. I
toss my cell phone aside and begin talking to my cats,

contemplating the world and these difficult times, meditating while focusing on my beautiful waterfall. Then again, I start wondering what am I doing here? This first day of silence is always the toughest one.

My cell phone chimes, and surprised to get a text on Sunday, I pick up the phone and read, "Hi, my name is Ron. We met in the airport about ten days ago. Do you remember me?"

A huge smile brightens my face. I still don't understand this new fad called texting; it seems like something to do when people have nothing else to do. Surprisingly, I decide to text back, "Yes, of course I remember you. How could I forget? What took you so long to contact me? ☺"

I toss the phone aside again; it chimes before it stops sliding across the table. I'm intrigued yet partially annoyed for the interruption of my thoughts, but also curious. I grab the phone to read, "I've been thinking about you and wanting to contact you since we met. How are you doing?"

I text back, "So you are thinking about me? Really? I'm fine. It was a long trip home, but happy to be here. It was a difficult week. What are you doing?"

Once more, I put the phone down, not expecting much more action, as it's after midnight wherever

he's texting from. But I find myself watching the phone to see if there is going to be another chime; I bet the kitties that the excitement is over for the day.

And yet, the chime comes again, "I am in Albuquerque at a golf tournament with some clients and colleagues. We've just finished dinner and having a few beers. Tell me about your week, maybe I can be of assistance."

REALLY? REALLY? This dude sitting in America, at a *golf* tournament, is going to tell me how to do my business…here?! How cute is that? But highly unlikely! "I have it under control, but thank you," I text back.

"Are you sure there isn't anything I may help you with? I have extensive experience in Indonesia and Africa to draw from," reads his follow-up text.

As we text back and forth over the next several hours, I am totally entertained. It is the wee hours of the morning where he is. I'm amazed that he managed to keep me interested and amused.

Then he texts, "Would you like to talk?"

Uhhh…uhhh…okaaayy, I'm thinking, this is startling. "Yes, I would. Sure, but it is very expensive to call here."

"No worries, let me gather up the gang and get back to the hotel, I'll call in about thirty minutes."

I am instantly on the internet with his business card in hand. He appears to be an executive for a large company that sells chemicals and expertise to the oil and gas industry. That sounds legitimate enough.

Once Ron calls, the conversation is as delightful and captivating as it was at the airport. A person I hardly know, fancies to hear the details and challenges thrust upon me *and* is actually offering advice and encouragement. No one else I know comprehends my life enough to inquire about it. This stranger is interested and eager to offer support and reinforcement. How delightful is that?! Of course there isn't anything that I take away as advice, but I don't let *him* know that. The conversation flows; it is enticing, not forced, and we laugh a great deal. Again, he has me smiling and charmed. I note that he once more deflects my questions about him, which makes me ask pointedly, "Are there any wives or kids I should know about?"

"Yes, I have two wonderful daughters."

"Really?" Thinking the shoe is about to drop, here it comes, "Tell me more."

"They are both grown and out of the house. Elise is the oldest and is a great girl. She has the most wonderful bubbly personality. Everyone that meets her just loves her. She is doing really well in her business in New Mexico. My younger daughter is well-educated; she has both her undergraduate and doctorate degrees in law from Baylor University. She is working at the District Attorney's office in Houston. I have big hopes for her."

"Oh, that's admirable. What happened with… their mom?"

"Well, it's a very unfortunate situation in which I dealt with for more than seventeen years…when I finally had to make some tough decisions."

"Is there a mental illness or an addiction involved?"

"Uh…yes, as a matter of fact, alcohol seems to be her best friend. You can't help someone that won't help herself. How did you know?"

"I've never heard anyone talk about divorce with compassion like you just did."

"Well, she is still the mother of my girls."

"My ex was an alcoholic as well, but there is no compassion coming out of my mouth in reference

to him. Before it was all over, I referred to him as the devil incarnate."

"Hmmm…were you married before you went to Indonesia?"

"No. I married a few years after I moved here."

"To an American or an Indonesian?"

"To an American. He was my boyfriend when my father took a turn for the worse; he broke up with me saying that he wasn't up for anything that heavy. We eventually got back together, unfortunately for me. But enough of that! Are you close to your girls?"

"Yes, I am. I'm very close to both, and I love them to death."

"Tell me more about them."

"My daughters have exact opposite personalities. They are precious, and we've been a fearsome trio sticking by each other through…well, a lot. I just tried to be the best father I could, no matter the circumstances or difficulties. We kind of grew up together."

"It sounds to me as if you took the job seriously."

"Yes, I did. I think they remember that and have always appreciated it." Ron tells me that it is 5:30 in the morning, and he needs to say good-bye, so he

will be able to get an hour of sleep before he tees off for the last day and round of golf. He had hoped his team would win the tournament. Once we hang up from each other, I wonder if I will ever hear from him again, probably not after he gets his phone bill!

Again, what's the use, why would he? Well, the kitties won the bet. I feed the kitties and me dinner and think how life proceeds as normal tomorrow, but *today* has been a truly enjoyable day!

5

How It All Began
August 1993

ali. Bali is where I plan to call home; it is a unique part of Indonesia. "When the first Dutch warship pulled into Bali in the late 16th century, the whole crew immediately jumped ship. It was heaven on earth. It took the captain two years to round up his men before he could set sail back to Holland. Bali is like one big sculpture. Every earthen step is manicured and polished, every field sculpted by hand. You can find Bali's soul towards the mountains. It is here that you will find rice paddies tripping down the hillsides like giant steps, holy mountains reaching up through the clouds, dense tropical jungles, long, sandy beaches, warm blue

water and crashing surf" (*Indonesian Handbook*). And it is here that I will encounter the extraordinary culture of the Balinese people, find myself and mend my soul.

Upon arriving, I don't take much time finding a bungalow and jeep for a long-term rental. I have never liked roach or mouse droppings, but now I learn about gecko droppings, as they're everywhere each morning. There is nothing like waking up in the middle of the night with a fifteen-inch grisly tropical lizard on the wall above your head calling out loudly, "GEC-KO! GECKKOO! GECKO!" The name originates from the loud nocturnal sound they make. I'm assured that I am lucky and blessed to have such creatures in my bungalow. I go along with this belief; it's not like I have a choice anyhow. I awake to the first breakfast in my own bungalow, where the house girl, Rumini, is ready to make me scrambled eggs and toast accompanied by fresh mango. I eat and sip my Bali coffee, also known as kopi, while adoring the way in which my bungalow sits on the edge of a deep volcanic ravine. My front porch sits among the treetops of the lush foliage growing from deep down inside the ravine. Coconuts, bananas, breadfruit, mangos, and other unknown fruits I cannot yet

identify are all reachable from my porch, right at the treetops. Numerous bright, beautiful multicolored birds, nearly within reach, serenade me in many different melodies as if saying, welcome to your new home and life here in Bali.

I am ready to bathe or mandi as referred to here. I call the houseboy who brings two buckets of hot water, or should I say barely warm by the time it gets to me, and pours it into a tiled basin, already partially filled with cool water. It makes the water ALMOST tolerable for bathing. I'm longing for an inviting hot shower but have no choice but to mandi, the same as the locals. I pour the first scoop of water over my head, and a loud, impulsive shriek escapes from my lungs and echoes throughout the mountains. The water feels very cold, considering the temperature outside is ninety-five degrees Farenheit. An equally loud shriek escapes with the second scoop of water. Shit, it's going to be a long time before I adjust to a mandi! The cold water is dripping from my body, and more of it is gushing from my long, thick hair that reaches down the middle of my back. Shit, shit, shit, it's cold!

I decide to begin the day with a peaceful walk through the monkey forest, as I haven't been there

yet. What could be more "Zen-like" than starting the day with a stroll through the forest admiring the natural wildlife? I fill my shoulder bag with peanuts and bananas as treats for the monkeys and start down the path. Gosh, the monkeys are everywhere; they do not seem to be shy either. I swear that a big one with gigantic balls is eyeing me and so is that one, and that one, and that one. I clear my throat rather loudly in hopes of backing the group away. I don't even get a little blink, just loud hissing and chatter from the group, several of them exposing their teeth. Look at the fangs on those guys! Now, I find myself completely surrounded by monkeys: big granddaddy-size ones all the way down to little bitty baby-size ones, and they are all still advancing toward me. I speak to them in a bold, lively voice, praying they will back down, "Hey there, dudes and dudettes, I'm new to the area and hope we can be friends. How are you doing today?"

Before I know what's happening, in quick lively motions, two monkeys scale my body, each sitting on a shoulder with their arms wrapped around my head and face. I stand there motionless, not knowing what to do. Partly in shock, partly in fear, and partly in amusement, laughter booms out from my

Satrece

soul, and tears start running down my face. I'm not certain if I am laughing so hard that I'm crying or if I'm crying so hard that I'm laughing. I remember the demonstration of their fangs and find myself thinking about whether or not they have rabies, or do they have fleas, lice, or something?

As I stand there in laughter and tears, my senses slowly start coming back to me, and I realize that my new friends want the treats in my shoulder bag. As I carefully and cautiously try to get to my stash, a brave monkey decides to climb up and sit on the top of my head while the other helps himself to the entire contents of my satchel. Peanuts, bananas, lipstick, keys, pen, calculator and my money are all being flung everywhere. Not knowing what to do, as one monkey still sits on my head, one on my shoulder, and now one is clinging around my waist, I work my way to a big stump and slowly sit down. As the food disappears, so does the interest in me, and finally, the monkeys begin to move on to their next prey. Whew, another day of survival.

It had been the recent death of my father that had initiated this journey. My father raised me, and I never much knew my mother. My father and I were very close. Simply put, Daddy got cancer and died,

though he fought it determinately every step of the way. It was a slow and painful death being eaten alive by several types of cancer. Talk about life knocking you upside the head. There's a time in your life, after both parents have left you, that you realize you are all alone in this world; there isn't one living or breathing soul who unconditionally loves you any longer. It's a life-changing experience. Life, as you know it, will never be the same. It's a period of reflection and reevaluation, it's a period of growth, aching growth, and even more pain, grief, and distress. It's a time of survival and a time of fear.

At the time, I had been working more than a hundred hours a week for nearly a decade. Having graduated from the University of Houston several years early, I was trying to prove myself as a professional woman in the 1980s in a man's business world. I started as a software engineer in a bank providing solutions to executive management, weaving through various positions that eventually culminated in a sales position providing high-tech solutions. But everything I knew and everything I had learned no longer made any sense to me after "the death."

A few of the words that I said at Daddy's eulogy summed it up:

"Daddy taught me most of what I know: how to be strong, but how to be me, how to work hard, how to set goals, and that I can be anything I wanted to be. He taught me to never settle for second best, nor to ever forget my vision.

But now I learn the most valuable lesson of all, and that is that today is my most precious possession."

Daddy's death left me in a state of misery, hope-lessness, and with a very heavy heart. Depression set in. The work that I had once loved now made for a day that I could hardly endure. Some people work to live, some people live to work. Now I was working just to live, trying to survive, and it wasn't going so well. I took a month off and went to Bali to "find" myself, to see if I could make sense of something again, of anything. Suddenly, my journey was launched. In pursuit of healing, purpose, and the universe's wisdom, I found myself living in Ubud, the soul of the island. What was normal life to the Balinese in 1993 is exactly what I needed. It is here that my journey began.

It's a tiny village in the mountains, where turning on my hair dryer to style the "BIG Texas hair" made it "the night the lights went out in Ubud," as far as the eyes could see. In denial and disbelief, I had to test it again the next night. Let's just say that

I threw the hair dryer into the trash, and after that, I didn't use another hair dryer for years to come.

Very quickly, I knew I had a lot to learn from Southeast Asia, like getting back to the basics of life. Life is not about power, control or materialistic things.

"It is only when you become totally concerned for the welfare of others, with complete commitment and simplicity and humility and humor...it is only when you take on the task of selfless giving and do it perfectly that real evolution occurs" (*Unplugging the Patriarchy*).

It's about having the ability to smile from the heart and tapping into the wisdom within. When one finds their life's purpose, the abundance will come. I watch Rumini make a blessing over the stove each day so she can cook me pleasing and healthy meals. She does the similar blessings at my Jeep, so I return home safely and then blessings at the front door of my bungalow so no bad demons or evil spirits will take hold. I enthusiastically embrace life's boundless possibilities with all of these blessings.

In Western societies, we create so many of our own stresses: the hunger for power and control, hierarchy and social status, and doing but not feeling,

thinking but not intuitively. Many Westerners focus on ourselves, not others, the world, or this wonderful universe we live in. Squatting on my haunches and having a conversation with the simplest Balinese, using a dictionary and many animated gestures of course, one can find more wisdom and happiness than I ever knew.

I needed to find some way to make an income while I tried to make sense of life so that I wouldn't completely exhaust my savings. On my first month-long trip, I started traveling throughout Indonesia seeking a way to make a few bucks to stay here. I eventually made my way to this most amazing little village on the northern coast of Java. Mahogany and teak woods are indigenous to this region. There were stacks and stacks of furniture stored on the side of the road. Most models were heavily carved Middle Eastern, Korean, and other Oriental models. The carving was awesome, beautiful, but the furniture construction and quality were suspect, and that's putting it nicely. Many of the models were so stunning, having some of the most exquisite, spectacular, three-dimensional relief carving I could imagine. There were these skinny, toothless, bare-chested men chewing on betel juice leaves, sitting on

workbenches near the roadside carving these woods. They smiled at me, looking at me as a novelty, but I couldn't help to notice how they looked at peace and worked with ease. Suddenly, I had my vision: utilize this wood, these remarkable carvers, and put them to work making Western furniture. My body tingled with excitement, and I felt like the hand of God had just been placed on my shoulder, assuring me that this was the next plan he had for me. I would use Western ingenuity and processes, a Western management style and Asian talent and resources. It would be an awesome match! It would be something spectacular! With this vision and little secret, I was armed and ready. But I first had to return to America to close out life as I knew it.

My mission began. Upon returning home, I put a nine-month business plan in place and proceeded with the essential tasks needed to make the vision a reality. I started by seeking a customer or customers to support me. Before I knew it, I had the interest and support of several people, *if* I can deliver on what I promised. I was intoxicated with hope and, with this plan, liquidated most of my assets, rid myself of possessions and placed a few remaining items in storage, just in case. I resigned from a six-figure-income

career and left the States as though my heels were on fire. My new life and journey began on August 23, 1993, a month earlier than my nine-month business plan stipulated.

I have begun my life in Bali!

I find the simple normal daily tasks not so normal nor so simple. Every day, new things titillate my senses. The sights, the sounds, the smells, the tastes are all different than what my mind and body are used to. Just running for groceries includes driving a Jeep on the wrong side of the road, shifting with my left hand, all the while seeming to be in a video game because bikes, scooters, cars, SUVs, people, buses, trucks, and ox carts are whirling at me from all directions and speeds. The Balinese always seem to be late, running on "rubber time," but when it involves driving, whether it is a scooter or a car, *get out of their way!*

Shopping includes an enormous amount of persistent hawkers spouting, "Berapa? Berapa? Berapa?" (How much will you give me for this?) Calculating in my head the exchange rate for each and every item is overwhelming. Trying to find something, anything, that I am familiar with for comfort, or that I just desire eating, is seldom successful. Filling the Jeep

with gas involves a few drums of fuel, a few boys sitting on the roadside, and an extraordinary syphoning effort of fuel from the drums. The syphoning effort, where they try to suck easy to not get the fuel in their mouth but always do, and spit and spat it out, always causes high drama; hence who could argue with whatever number comes to their mind for payment. The cost is based on a guesstimate of how much fuel is remaining in the drum. Who can argue with the fuel boys, who have such a perilous career. I accept their charge, the first of many things I learn to accept, and go on my way.

A few days a week, I go from the mountains to the ocean, to Legian-Seminyak Beach for a long swim in the beautiful ocean and to further satisfy my addiction to scorching my skin in the extraordinarily hot tropical sun. There are over six miles of coastline on the Indian Ocean here, the only thing beyond is the continent of Australia, which is more than a thousand miles away. This area is the home of many expats seeking the incessant party and social scene, parading their masterfully created tattoos and copious piercings, unlike most of the expat inhabitants of Ubud, who are seeking privacy, healing or soulful enlightenment. As I stand on the beach gazing into

the infinite waters, the ocean continues calling my name. I enter the water until I'm thigh deep, dive and swim to the ocean floor with my eyes open, admiring the blue waters that I'm immersed in, sensing the merciless currents and waves rolling above that will soon crash into the shoreline. I carefully time the water so that when surfacing for air, I'm not slapped in the face by the monstrous waves. I swim out past the break line, and I swim and I swim. One minute I imagine I'm a dolphin gliding through the vast waters, and the next, I dive as deep as I can and imagine I'm a cavorting mermaid. After I'm exhausted, I swim back to the swells and frolic. I wait for the imposing swells to come and toss me high into the air several times and eventually ride a wave into shore. I lay on a sarong tanning my exhausted body while gazing at the high seas. I hunger for so much more than just marveling at the ocean or swimming and diving. This day quenches my hunger for the moment, but soon, the appetite for more surges. I must tear myself away from my fixation with the seas each time I return to the mountains of Ubud.

During my time on Bali, I explore more of the island, sometimes traveling to the east coast's Candidasa-Padang Bai area where I rent a two-story

bungalow for $19 a night that sits twenty feet from the ocean. I spend time snorkeling and scuba diving the Tulamben wreck of the *USS Liberty*, all the time learning how to be self-sufficient, capable, and competent on the island.

While at home, the sunset brings serenity to me as I learn more and more lessons each day. Soon, there will be the small glow of candles and one little lamp lighting the bungalow as it sits open upon the ravine, bringing nature onto my porch. Rumini lets down the mosquito net for the night and strategically places mosquito coils. The sounds of the night will slowly but surely break through the evening silence. It is here that I spend each night recalling the events of the day, laughing at myself for the various *faux pas*, and eventually beginning to count my blessings, one by one.

6

Intro to Jepara 101
Java 1993

*I*t's now October. Once I learned to adequately maneuver around Bali, it is time to head to Java and get the wheels of progress moving. My business plan is to start slowly, a step-by-step process. I will begin by ordering products from an existing factory using my designs and incorporating my quality control instructions. This will help me to begin learning the ropes. Having access to beautiful and exotic mahogany wood, it only seems appropriate to first follow design ideas along the infamous Chippendale "ball and claw" line.

Indonesia is a country of incredible and diverse beauty. It stretches across one-seventh of the globe

between Malaysia and Australia, and it is a strategic location straddling both waterways between the Pacific and Indian oceans. It is comprised of over 17,500 islands. Also straddling the equator, Indonesia is the fourth-largest country in the world by population, about 220 million people. This is more than the combined population of all the other Southeast Asian countries. Still considered a Third World country, Indonesia has an estimated per capita income of about $520 a year. Nationwide, more than 35 percent of the workforce is unemployed.

Most Indonesians live and die within the site of a volcano. This area is known as the Ring of Fire. It has about four hundred volcanoes, and approximately seventy to eighty of them are still active. All this volcanic activity that destroys also aids growth and life again. Its past eruptions have left some of the most fertile land in the world. You can plant a stick in the ground and it will sprout leaves and crops. Four-out-of-five Indonesians work the soil. It's one of the world's largest producers of rubber, rice, and coffee. Indonesia sits on the largest and richest oil reserves in Southeast Asia. It has the largest tropical forest reserves in the world after the Amazon and is richer

Satrece

in plant species than most all other places combined. This is an amazing place!

My flight into Surabaya connects onward to Semarang. It's about 110 degrees Fahrenheit in the busy, stifling and noisy airport. Everybody in this small airport is moving with purpose, but each and every one manages to take time to stare at me with wonderment and contemplation. No one speaks English. Supposedly a two-hour layover, four hours pass, and I'm still sitting in the small plastic chairs drinking a room-temperature Coke, wondering if I missed my flight. I keep showing my boarding pass to airport employees, and they all keep saying "Nanti, nanti" or "later," as my dictionary informs me.

Finally, I arrive in Semarang, and I'm accosted by the masses, all shouting and offering their trans- portation or hotels, cheap ones or lovely ones. Other people are calling, "Transport, transport!" I slowly work my way through the crowds and hire a metered taxi to take me to Jepara. It is here that I learn my next new words for the day, "Sopir, lebih pelan, silakan. Lebih pelan!" I am demanding, "Driver, slow down, please. Slow down!" After four hours of hanging on for dear life in eight lanes of traffic on two lanes of road and five million honking horns

distraction

with drivers who are driving on the shoulders of the road, nearly killing motorcyclists which carry their entire family of four and five people, and avoiding eight near-death situations ourselves, we arrive at the hotel. I'm exhausted, and my nerves are frazzled. *I am totally spent.*

I had reserved the suite at $13 a night, and I was assured that it was the nicest room anywhere around, thus giving me hope. Using my dictionary and many hand gestures, I learn the room isn't available; the previous occupant hasn't left as scheduled. As determination sets in, I continue clumsily communicating with a smile on my face, a kind and sincere look in my eyes and a pleasant voice from my lips. My hopes are that a smile, combined with my charm and persistence, will win. A deal is a deal, and honor is honor; this reservation had been made long ago and recently confirmed. After a long while and not giving up, I am told to wait. I eventually find out that the person in the room acknowledges their overstay and is packing to move rooms. Yes! I win, the first of many victories, I expect.

I sit in the little hotel restaurant while waiting for my room to be prepared, and I order an orange juice only to receive a room-temperature orange Fanta. Oh

well, I smile. I probably need to get used to it; this will be my life for a while. I decide to compile a notepad of word translations from my dictionary that I will need during this trip, as no one speaks English in this remote place. I'm finally being escorted to my room, and I'm filled with pride that I was smart enough to reserve it and have been persistent enough to get it. I know that it has air-conditioning and a television, so how bad can it be? I walk in, look around at the room, and all I want to do is cry. How much more can I endure today? However, I can't. I can't allow the room boy to see my disappointment because he is so proud to present this room to me, and I had fought so indiscriminately for it. It is a room about 120 square feet in size, and the light above the bed is a wire hanging from the ceiling with a twenty-watt lightbulb. It does have an air conditioner that, however, is hardly cooling, and the room is nearly the same temperature as it is outside. The AC unit drips copious amounts of water into large puddles on the floor and is so filthy that I fear I will have a viral infection before I depart. I sit on the bed and look around the room. The bed is made with one polyester sheet, two flat-foam pillows, and one worn, thin ikat blanket. The walls and tile floor are stark white

with mosquitos filling and swarming the room. I'm flapping and swinging my arms to fight the swarms. The toilet doesn't flush but has a bucket of water with a scooper to manually flush it and, of course, no toilet paper. Neither is there a lamp to read by, and reading is my survival tool. I turn on the television, and as expected, the only English-speaking channel is CNN International. Unfortunately, in its infancy stages, the programming lasts for about forty-five minutes and repeats.

Knowing that this is "home" for at least the next two weeks, I methodically start making it livable. I ask for a can of Baygon spray to kill the mosquitos, clean the air-conditioning filter and begin to unpack, including my extra rolls of toilet paper that I had so smartly brought with me. I proceed to get ready for bed as I have a big day tomorrow and it's the official start of my new business. I quickly fall asleep from the trying day, but in the night when I roll over, the bed breaks and the mattress and I slam through to the floor. The left side of the mattress is still remaining in place in the frame, while the right side of the mattress lies on the floor, and which, of course, includes me. Exasperated, I get up to fix the bed and am successful in maneuvering the mattress

back into the frame. Shortly, I manage to fall to sleep again, and abruptly, I'm hurled as the mattress and I join the floor once again. I remove the mattress from the bed frame and lay it on the floor in the middle of the frame, as the mosquitos swarm. I crawl onto the mattress disheartened and pull the sheet up over my head and sleep as best I can for the rest of the night.

The next morning, I order a taxi but, to my dismay, learn that there are no taxis serving the area. Semarang is the closest place with taxis, the place I had come from the day before, which might as well be as far away as the moon at this moment. Well, okay, I tell myself, I will be better off with a car and driver anyway. Car and driver? With the blank stares I receive, I soon learn that "car and driver" doesn't exist either. After more patience and persistence, the desk clerk is now saying, "Maybe I can find my friend …" I end up in a minivan that has been used to herd goats and learn that air-conditioning is *not* needed to herd goats. Note to self: in the future, ask and clarify that the car has air-conditioning. The rest of the day is about as successful as finding my initial taxi.

I continue to work the transportation issues over the next few days and finally find an accept-

able-enough car and driver. The vehicle is at least eight years old, still with no air-conditioning, but with mud from their goats and ripped seats. But I'm assured that the engine is sound. We continue to go from factory to factory looking for the best factory to make my designs. Though still highly infatuated with the wood and carving, the furniture-making skills are vastly inferior, with the color finishing including dust, insects, and drip marks throughout. As day after day passes, I'm now ending up at open-structured buildings at the end of dirt roads, all known as furniture-producing factories. The quality has only gotten unbelievably worse. I've made no progress whatsoever.

After my allotment of time in Jepara without any success, I decide to return to Bali. I need rest, a decent meal and civilization. This will allow me to think more clearly. Java is harsh and laborious; it has been difficult and demanding. I learn I'm not as well-prepared as I thought. I need to understand the language better and the culture a little more, and just maybe, my plan needs tweaking.

Initial score: Java – 1, Satrece – 0.

7

The Surprise Call
May 2008

"**W**ell, this call is a pleasant surprise."

"I'm glad that's how you see it," Ron says, relieved.

"You must not have received your phone bill to be calling me again," Satrece jokes.

"Aahhh, I'm not worried about that. I see that you aren't big on texting, huh? You sometimes leave me hanging for days. I often wonder if you'll ever text me back. And not a big e-mailer either?"

"Uh, well…gosh, I have A LOT going on right now, but if it makes you feel any better, your texts always bring a smile to my face…and your e-mails are always refreshing too."

"Well, that's good to hear, and it certainly does make me feel better. You had left me wondering; at least that gives me hope."

"Hope for what?"

"What would you say if I told you that I've planned a business trip to Indonesia, and I would like to ask you out on a date? Perhaps the second week of June?" Ron says with excitement and confidence.

"Uh, well, I would say that you should have spoken to me before you planned a trip here. I'm unavailable that week," Satrece says reluctantly into the phone while feeling surprised.

Ron gasps at the other end of the phone, "What? Why?" He exclaims, "What could you possibly be doing in the jungle to be unavailable for the entire week?"

"If you'll recall when we met, I told you that my brother would be visiting soon. On the fifteenth of this month, I fly to Jakarta to meet him and bring him home with me. I figured after three weeks here, he would need a break, so I've planned and paid in advance for us to go to Bali that week, and it's nonrefundable."

"Oh, I see. Well, I guess I could go to Bali to see you."

"UHH, I didn't exactly invite you," Satrece says, smiling but confused. "This is for my brother and me to spend some time together. I've hardly seen him in fifteen years."

"Hmmm. Well, I guess I need to get busy and see if I can reschedule my business meetings. I presently have everything lined up perfectly," Ron sighs, "but I'll see what I can do. So how about the third week in June, are you available then?"

"No. There is no way I can fly to Jakarta to meet you then either," Satrece says meekly.

"Well, why not?" Ron asks, incredulous. Was he being shunned?

"If I spend the week in Bali, I'll need to work the week I return to Jepara. This is actually a very bad time for me to even be going to Bali, but I need to do this for my brother's welfare. I can't simply return and abandon my brother and my business during these challenging times by running off to Jakarta… to go out on a *date* with you." *Good grief, the thought of that word, DATE, haunts me.* "I do own a business, you know, and it actually does require me to work," Satrece states sternly.

"Well, IF I can change my meetings, can you possibly take some time the *LAST* week of June?" Ron asks, dismayed.

"Well, I suppose…I can do a quick trip to Jakarta during that week. After all, if you come this far, the least I can do is be hospitable; I would enjoy dinner with you. Sure, if you can change your meetings, I will figure out a way to make it," Satrece says, not too assuredly but adding a soft laugh.

"I cannot believe that I planned a trip to the other side of the world as a surprise for you, and you can hardly make any time for me …" Ron pouts and fades out, leaving Satrece to defend herself even further.

Ron hangs up the phone that morning knowing it's nighttime in Asia Pacific, and there's nothing that he can do for twelve more hours in an attempt to rearrange his schedule. He contemplates the phone call and Satrece. He *will* find a way to rearrange his meetings; he *will* see Satrece again. As Ron thinks about her exquisite beauty, he cannot stop thinking about her tall, voluptuous body and long legs. She is damn intoxicating to him. He remembers how difficult it was to break her barriers at the airport, but he also remembers her genuine warmth and the shine

that twinkled from her eyes once he finally did. He'd wanted to get lost in her stare with her radiant eyes and the bewitching mysteriousness that shadows her. Ron hadn't counted on a woman so intriguing being so frustrating and obstinate, which makes him just that much more determined in his quest. This woman is going to haunt him until they meet again.

Satrece, in total astonishment, looks at her cats, all of whom are staring at her in bewilderment, as they aren't used to hearing the odd sound that has come to her voice. She exhales. "So what do you make of this, kitties? I didn't see this one coming. He thinks just because he has business on this side of the world, I'm supposed to drop everything and go running, not to mention, flying to meet him? Whewww! Doesn't he understand that a business owner just can't drop everything, and for a date? Of course he does; he was quite understanding under the circumstances. The timing of his visit is just horrible though; you think he understands that?"

The cats blink, and then they yawn, very unconcerned with the whole matter. As I return to reading my book, my concentration is fully blown. I realize that his expectations of me flying away to meet him in such bad timing has left me a bit annoyed. The

last thing I need at this moment is extra pressure. However, I can't help but be profoundly impressed that he has the means to get to Indonesia and so soon. He certainly is a man of his word. So far, from my first glimpse of him, he has proven himself to be the man that I had gauged. Yes, successful and confident, in control and determined, I think, as I close my eyes and ponder him more. I wonder what it would be like to be held in his arms, for his athletic arms to engulf me tenderly, pulling me close to him, to smell his scent. I remember his light-hearted demeanor and his charismatic aura, yet his intense stares, as if he were searching the depths of my being. Yes, I've been stared at, even gawked at, but he looked at me with so much fervor. He studied my every move and hung on to my every word.

Two days later, about the same time at night, the phone rings again.

After all the kind greetings, Ron states proudly, "Well, it wasn't easy, but I did it."

"What is it that you were able to do, Ron?"

"I was able to change all of my meetings, and I pushed everything back two weeks. So based on your word, I guess I will be seeing you the last week of June," Ron muses.

With astonishment, Satrece stutters, "Huh, what? Uh, well, okay then. Then it's confirmed…it's a date."

Though I'm already impressed with his abilities, I hadn't thought he'd be able to change his entire schedule. What's a girl to do now? "Yes, it *is* a date."

"I'll be in the Asia Pacific area working the weeks prior, so we'll work out the details once I'm in the region. Is that okay with you?"

Satrece agrees to the plan, and this gives her more time to see how things progress with the business and her brother.

"By the way, there's something else you should know," urges Ron gently.

I hesitate, and I'm definitely afraid to ask.

"What is it?"

"Well, if I'm traveling all that distance, motivated by my desire to see you, I've decided to take some vacation time. I'll be there an additional week in hopes of getting to know you better."

Holy freakin' shit! The balls on this dude!

8

Ron Enters the War Zone on All Fronts

R on's father died from a heart attack when he was eleven. He was the youngest of six children, raised in the small town of Beach, North Dakota, just miles from the Montana border. His father had been a well-respected police chief in their community, and before he left this world, he ensured that Ron understood honor, dignity, and hard work. Ron was basically on his own from the age of eleven. His mom did her best to raise him, but it was his sister Staci who had the major impact in his life. She taught him right from wrong and good from bad, and he had her unwavering support.

Ron worked exceptionally hard to become who he was, for everything that he acquired in his life and everything that he accomplished. Like everyone in the Midwest during his young adulthood, he married young but still managed to work his way through college. As a matter of fact, he was the first in the family to graduate from a university. Ron was determined to make the best of life and make something of himself. Coming from a poor family without resources, no real guidance concerning education, career opportunities and the like, he'd need find his own way. He only had himself to rely on to be successful and to discover how to enjoy the entire splendor that this great world could provide, and maybe someday find true love with a wonderful woman.

Ron was on a work assignment in Indonesia with his family when he realized that his wife had serious alcohol problems, and that she was not the woman of his dreams. It was her insistence that led them to return to the United States and seek his next assignment. His two delightful daughters, Elise and her younger sister, and he would have been elated to remain in Indonesia or welcome another international assignment. But Ron believed that if his family were Stateside, he could get help and support for his

wife's issues. Unfortunately, she refused to admit to any such problem or the plight of her situation, so it grew into a state of inflating challenges. Ron made the necessary changes in his family dynamics and chose to love and support his children and to return to the States.

Having his hands full with all of this, he did his best to create a normal family life for the girls. From his desire to be a good father and give his daughters unwavering attention in all that they did, Ron went to great lengths to provide wonderful homes and to be a distinct and encouraging influence in their lives. They had a strong bond that seemed unbreakable. All the while, he discreetly hid his distaste that resulted from his wife's degrading behavior.

The following six years were spent in New Orleans and in Denver, and both were fun and wonderful cities. However, his marriage continued to deteriorate, and at that same time, his career began suffering. Ron saw no future in his diminishing relationship so seized control of his life for self-preservation. He had to make a decision that things had to change with or without his wife's support. So they relocated to Houston, Texas, where he accepted an assignment in West Africa to further advance

his experience and career. He commuted between Houston and Nigeria, including the rest of the West African countries, so was frequently gone for long durations of three-to-five weeks at a time.

It was in West Africa that Ron experienced all that you would not wish upon anyone, friend or foe. Numerous times, he was held at gunpoint; and once he was caught in a shoot-out in the jungle, yet Ron had the calm demeanor to negotiate peace between both sides. Another time, he thought he would be shot out of the air by surface-to-air missiles directed at his helicopter. This was just another day in the life of living in West Africa. Ron began thinking that maybe a life focused on his career can have its draw-backs too? Wouldn't romance and a scantily dressed woman be more desirous about now?!

The hotel accommodations in West Africa reminded him of the remote places in Indonesia; however they were much worse. Ron worked long days seldom having a palatable meal, much less a healthy one. He contracted malaria twice, once get-ting himself to Frankfurt, Germany before he col-lapsed in the hotel room for days in an attempt to medically treat himself. Self-healthcare is often the best alternative in West Africa; however, the med-

ications he had taken nearly killed him. He literally wanted to die.

Ron found that his talents allowed him to relate to all levels of society from the leaders of the countries to the common person. He was fearless in creating access, leading and directing African agencies to success in their projects while creating a better life for all of the nationals who were employed by his company for which he was also leading.

Once, while in Nigeria, the Nigerian owner of their joint-venture partnership, Eddy, and Ron were traveling from Port Harcourt to Eket. While in transit, they were stopped by a roadblock controlled by a temporary office placed on the roadside complete with government officials from the immigration department. As is normal in corrupt countries like Nigeria, the officials wanted *monetary assistance* that, of course, he would not, nor could not, ever agree to. The U.S. government takes this type of *barter* seriously. There are strict ethical standards to maintain, and the sentence for such atrocities is serious. Eddy was highly offended at the officers' request, thus an active discussion prevailed.

Suddenly, machine guns, with fingers on the triggers, were pointed at them, and their security

detail followed suit with an even larger arsenal of their own. *What in the hell does he do now?!* Insults were thrown amid screaming orders from both sides; a pistol was drawn by Eddy, and he actually placed it at the head of the lead immigration officer! At this point, Ron had no choice but to step in and stop all of the foolishness before someone was seriously injured or killed. After a calm, cool, collective discussion, he successfully brought peace to the situation; and eventually, they continued on their journey. He thought to himself, *I'm one cool cat to have maintained order in this dangerous predicament, how did I pull that off?* This was just one of many times to come.

On another occasion, Ron was in Lagos crossing the bridge from Victoria Island to Lagos mainland in a company-driven vehicle. While in heavy traffic, called a "go slow," a large truck and trailer stopped in front of them, seeming to have engine trouble. The car behind them pulled in very close; the traffic on both sides of them was so heavy that it was impossible to make any advance. Within seconds, the car engine of the Peugeot that he was in just stopped. Then he saw someone climbing out from beneath the car; their fuel line was disconnected, literally

within seconds! The car was paralyzed. His team had been set up!

Six men inclusive with clubs and knives began beating on the car and demanding money, computers, and any and all items of value in the car. "Oh shit, GANGSTERS!" Typically, Ron carries a minimum of US$5,000 because when traveling in these environments, credit cards aren't of much use, and fraudulent charges likely will show up on your card within hours of your first transaction. He'd learned this lesson the hard way more than once in the amount of hundreds of thousands of dollars. And this was the first time in a long time that he didn't have a security detail with him. Normally, he always traveled with at least one armed guard, complete with machine gun, pistols, and a bulletproof vest. But this day, it was the driver, a Public Relations Officer named Onabanjo, an American colleague and him.

The driver exited the car in hopes to ease this dangerous situation, but he was nearly beaten to death. Onabanjo is a wiry man of slight stature, and other than his phenomenal knowledge and ability to make stuff happen, he also believes that he can calm any situation. Against Ron's guidance, he got out of the car. He too was taken to the ground and

was beaten profusely. Aside from him, there was the other American dude, and he was terrified and panic-stricken and simply beside himself.

Ron figures he thrives on *living on the edge* because he wasn't fazed by the situation, *but maybe this was a bit too much?* Why wasn't he embraced in the arms of a beautiful woman kissing her luscious lips right then instead of this dreadful assignment that kept aiming to get him killed? Ron ascertained which thug was the leader and demanded that he speak with *him and only him.* After some persuasion and a threat, "I don't care about the others, and if you want something out of this, you have to talk to me," the head thug opened a dialogue. Ron convinced the thug to make this about him. While promising to help him get something out of this, he explained that the other gentlemen didn't have anything to give, so please just let them go. The thug bought it! Ron was effective in his negotiations with the gangsters. Within twenty minutes, the situation was diffused without him leaving the the car. He only lightened his wallet by a few dollars. Having developed trust and a relationship with the gangster, the deal was done, and they were leaving. Then Ron quickly demanded one more thing: "Reconnect the gas line." With the others in the car still shaken, he

calmly says to them, "It's all how you handle things," yet thinking *whew, my dad must still be looking over me.* They eventually proceeded on their way.

Yet another dangerous West African work situation unfolded when a colleague and Ron had finished their business in the Niger Delta, a well-known area of Nigeria known for its large reserves of crude oil and natural gas. As with most oil and gas fields, the area is extremely remote, only reachable by fixed-wing aircraft or helicopter or by speedboat, which means a three-and-a-half to four-hour journey on a dangerous river inhabited by pirates. The next flight out was still a few days off, but they had no intention of waiting that long. Ron had a close relationship with the management of the oil company they were working with, so he secured a helicopter, allowing them to be on their way. The next destination was a large village named Warri. Out of the fifty-to-fifty five countries he had worked in, Warri, Nigeria IS the end of the world. The only way to understand what a shithole this place was is to see it firsthand. And just the night before on CNN, he had seen fires, the aftermath of numerous bomb explosions and dead bodies with severed heads being clearly displayed by terrorists as trophies as well as many other atrocities;

for him, it's just another trip to Warri. As they were about to board the helicopter, he was pulled to the side by the friend who helped him secure the aircraft, and Paul asked him, "Is it okay if I put a few passengers on this flight with you?"

"Sure," responded Ron and was pleased to be of help but then noticed the passengers were Nigerian Special Forces locked and loaded for battle.

The logistics manager whispered, "It's possible you will be shot at with rocket launchers; not because they don't like you, but they want to get to your new friends."

Although the true purpose of this twenty-minute flight was for Ron and his colleague to get to their next destination in a timely manner, a new twist had been thrown into the plot. The gentlemen joining their flight were to land in Warri and crush fresh uprisings in process. Like them, they needed a ride. Ron also learned that some sympathizers for one warring faction were in charge of flight coordination and transportation; hence, they were the perfect decoys for this mission. As they approached Warri, it became obvious that the fighting was fierce, and the threat of being shot out of the air was real! Thankfully, no

rockets were fired at their helicopter. It was a tense time not knowing if he would live or die.

Dealing with governments, state and national politics, rules and regulations, in addition to the corruption that goes with doing business in West Africa, made it one of the most difficult and challenging assignments. Ron had to stay one step ahead of the locals in every transaction, doing his best to anticipate what they were thinking before they thought it. Sometimes, it was so challenging that it took you to the edge before you could overcome the situation. You couldn't even make this stuff up; after all, it's West Africa! Through all of this, Ron built a thriving, profitable, and sustainable business. He often did business here with executives from Fortune 100 companies and ran with top political leaders, including vice presidents of the nations where he worked and traveled. Wouldn't it be wonderful to have the love of his life escorting him while he met with dignitaries or at least have that special woman waiting for his arrival home from these perilous missions?

Ron found the experience of traveling to these strange and unique places around the world to be remarkably rewarding. He had to outmaneuver and conquer challenging situations, advancing his com-

pany's position as he shaped its relations with heads of state and dignitaries. Ron was responsible for developing infrastructure in these nations, creating jobs, training nationals—all the while laying a foundation for the future of the locals and the success of his company. He was blessed with this unique honor.

In many countries, such as Angola, Ron witnessed horrific poverty. He made a difference and helped where he could. In other countries, he was often one of the first people sent in to build the business; he was the second person to enter Equatorial Guinea for the company. It was a full-time job avoiding the corrupt immigration officials who demanded large amounts of money, otherwise sending you to jail. Again, it was an incredible opportunity for Ron to be able to see and witness the fruits of his efforts, watch them grow and turn them into successes.

The hotels were horrific. Often, he found himself sleeping in his clothes in a chair or on top of the bed in what was said to be the nicest hotel in the country so that he wouldn't get bitten by bed bugs or other creatures that roamed the room. But he still made the best of these daunting assignments. His teams and he were abundantly fulfilled while explor-

ing this part of the world and creating a successful legacy for others to follow. And he actually survived!

One may never know to meet him that he'd had these extraordinary experiences in such overly challenging and dangerous places. Upon meeting Ron, people assume he is merely a "city boy," as he is considered a true gentleman and polished. However, through it all, he's maintained his strong ethics, morals and character, performing this role with poise and stature. He sleeps well at night.

Ron had hoped that in his absence, his wife would find her courage and strength; but on the contrary, the family situation became more dire. He tried everything conceivable to handle the plight, only to learn that if someone doesn't think there's a problem and doesn't want help, there's not much one can do. Ron concluded the assignment in West Africa to spend more time at home where he was clearly needed.

Being a devout Catholic, he never believed in divorce. As years passed, the circumstances continued to worsen and grew more critical, eventually leaving him to grow emotionally detached from his wife and not really caring if they repaired their relationship or not. He went about his life but still remained a faith-

ful and good husband. Frequently—often, almost always—he dreamed of love and happiness with that special woman. He knew she was out there; he just needed to be freed and given the opportunity to find her. It's his lifelong dream for happiness, romance and love. Is that too much to ask? It has to be out there, somewhere, doesn't it?!

Ron spent his spare time with the girls making certain they were faring through the trauma of dealing with a dysfunctional parent. He also held several elected and appointed positions for various councils within the community and church organizations. It could be said that he threw himself into his work and all the hobbies and sports that he could handle.

Ron decided that once both girls were out of the house and had their own successful lives, he had to follow his true heart; he deserved happiness, and more important, he aspired to have true love. He wanted the life that he had always dreamed of. With much soul-searching and consultations with his priest, he made the tough heart-wrenching decision and finally opted for divorce. Is SHE really out there, that perfect, special woman? Will I find her? If she is, will she understand me, my desires with my crazy world and all of who I am?

9

Black Magic and Tigers for Satrece in 1994

My first forty-foot container of mahogany Chippendale-like furniture has just been loaded and is off to the port of Semarang. It's shipped from Semarang to Singapore through the South China Sea, where it will be loaded onto the next container ship to travel the Pacific Ocean into Long Beach, California. Then it will be placed on double-stacked trains and sent onward to my customer. It has been approximately nine months since my efforts to begin this business.

I meet Huda, a local Javanese who has connections, speaks English well enough and is knowledgeable about the furniture business. Huda is anx-

ious to start his own business but doesn't have the funds. I offer him five percent of my company, and he accepts. We collaborate and launch a new business quickly by building a supervising team. I select the best of the best from factories I had visited, of course choosing these people with Huda's blessing. It was clear to me which factories used the best wood, had the best carvers, the best furniture-making skills, brass and glass installation, quality finishing, upholstery, packing, etc. These are the factories from where I recruited my supervisors.

Once our team was in place, they chose the workers they wanted, and the workers just began showing up. First, there were five, then the next week there were twenty, and then there were forty and so on, all unbeknownst to me where they were coming from. The first container of furniture had been produced with one of those "open structured buildings at the end of a dirt road" that we had rented as we slowly acquired the tools, workers, and materials needed to produce. Meanwhile, I started looking for a more permanent place for a factory.

I had returned time and time again to Jepara from Bali until one day, I just didn't leave. I was still living in the $13 suite at the Ratu Shima Hotel while

this entire first container was produced with our own workers. While living at the Ratu Shima, I meet an Australian of Hungarian descent named Atos. To my astonishment, I learn that Atos has a large factory here in Jepara and is quite successful using a business plan similar to mine with one exception: he is shipping his containers to his partner in Australia to be sold in Australia. I also learn that he already has two other Westerners working for him, both from Australia. The infrastructure in Jepara is still so basic, the Ratu Shima is the only place in town to eat and drink. Atos and his two colleagues show up for dinner and beer, lots of beer, nearly every night. I eventually begin to dine with them. As we eat our fried rice, mie goreng, or chicken schnitzel, they drink the Bintang beer. Each night, they share a new story on how to or how not to do whatever it is that challenged me for the day. They are a total blessing and my entertainment.

The remote life quickly shows on Atos and his guys. From the moment I meet them, I see that these people smoke and drink too much, don't eat in a healthy way nor get enough sleep, revealed by their red-rimmed eyes and pallid skin. On one occasion at dinner, they all show up black and blue, some

with busted eyes, some with busted lips, and one with both. They are covered with cuts and bruises, so when I inquire what has happened, thinking the worst, I learn merely that they forcefully fought with each other the previous night over local girls. After further inquiries, I learn that the brawl is over girls named Fitra, Sheila, and a sister of Fitra. This all has something to do with one of the girls being fourteen years old, boundaries crossed and jealousies among the group. I decide that it's better that I don't know the details, and maybe it is best that I stay away from them. The next night, they arrive with the young girls in tow. The fourteen-year-old is toting a Cinderella backpack, and the oldest one is sixteen. It is very clear that these girls are being courted; these girls seem to be treated well and soon become their wives.

The next week, the guys have burn marks up and down their arms, and again after my inquiries, I learn they held a contest to see who could hold a matchbook of burning matches to their flesh the longest. It never ceases to amaze me what Bintang beer and isolation makes them do. I soon decide that I will have dinner in my room to distance myself from my new friends.

While living at the Ratu Shima, I meet an Englishman named Carlton who also has a furniture factory in Jepara. He is a tall, lanky character who always seems to have a smile on his face. Carlton is instrumental in helping me find a home. As a matter of fact, he had modified a factory for his home and is now moving to something bigger and better, making his home available. Having acquired this place from Carlton, I now call it home. It is a partial indoor-outdoor structure with several buildings inside, surrounded by twelve-foot walls, making it a compound. Carlton had added three feet of barbed wire on top of the walls for security. The compound has a room for a bedroom, a room for an office, a place for a toilet and a mandi area on teak deck floors, and an area with a counter that can be set up as a kitchen. The compound, with the exception of the two rooms, has nothing more than a lean-to roof, making the rest of the area pavilion living. A good portion of the compound has no roof at all, making it an under-the-stars garden living space. The one thing I can say is that it does have character! Also, this compound is within five hundred meters of two different mosques, which I am told makes it a blessed home. Carlton was also upgrading to a larger

factory, which allowed me to take over the lease on his first factory. The second round of blessings has now been bestowed upon me. Business is successful for the other Western factories in Jepara, which encourages me. With my first container in transit, I suddenly feel like a trusted and proven pro.

"Huda, now that I have some experience and my Bahasa is coming along, I'm ready to take on more daily responsibilities. I've been thinking…now is a good time for me to begin managing the workers," I say.

Huda shrugs and says, "Yeah, okay, if that's what you want, Ms. Satrece. Do you want to begin today? There are two workers who want to meet with me. Should I call one of them in now to see what he wants?"

"Sure, why not?"

As the first worker enters, he only speaks in a local Javanese dialect, and I need Huda to interpret. The employee says that his grandmother is very ill, and he needs to borrow money, so she can go to the hospital. As customary, we can cut his wages each pay period until his loan is repaid in full. *Since I have become so smart in the local ways*, I know to tell him that

I will take this into consideration and will advise him after I have had time to think about it.

We then call in the next person, and again, Huda has to interpret. The young man tells us with such gravity that this morning his uncle has been turned into a tiger, and he needs money immediately to have a special ceremony to save him. I first listen in puzzlement to this entertaining story, then do my best to suppress a smile, asking him for more details. He begins telling us how his uncle disappeared last night and hasn't come home. This morning, an extremely large tiger entered into his village with tatters of his uncle's shirt hanging from him. He proceeds to tell us that the tiger was captured and is being held at the local police station. He and Huda have lots of additional conversation over this. I am absolutely certain that this person is taking a run at me and/or us. As I dismiss this person, I turn to Huda, smiling, and say, "Well, this is an easy one. I support helping the grandmother, and though I really adore tigers, I don't see financing them. Is that the way you see it?" I knew my decision was a sound one.

Huda begins, "Uhhh, Ms. Satrece, I know the grandmother very well...she is my neighbor. And I also know that she is not ill; I spoke with her only

this morning. I guess this employee is taking a run at us to see what our management style is going to be. And uh…uh…his uncle *did* turn into a tiger. It's the talk of the town. I went by the prison this morning on my way to work to see it, and the tiger was wearing the shirt of his uncle." I sit staring at Huda, incredulously sensing that he believes this with all of his heart.

"So…does this happen often? People turning into tigers? How can this be? Tell me more …"

"This is the first time I have seen it myself, but I have heard many stories similar to this. This is black magic, and it's very powerful in this area. The heart of the black magic is from the island of Madura, just east of here. The man obviously crossed someone to have this put upon himself. He is a good man. We must help him in any way and soon." I had already heard early on from Atos that Indonesians believe in black magic through and through, and I don't see any option other than to go along with their beliefs, at least this once. We finance the tiger ceremony.

The next morning as Huda enters into the factory, he hands me a local newspaper. Headlines read in Bahasa, "The Local Police Capture Tiger, Man Missing." The story supports the same dissertation

revealed to me the day before. I learn that today, the tiger will be sent to the Semarang jail for holding while it awaits a special shaman from Madura to reverse the spell. The family of the missing man will go to Semarang to see that the man tiger is sufficiently taken care of. Needless to say, I decide that Huda is better equipped to manage the daily needs of the workers while I continue to manage the business, the furniture, the customers, and the finances. For the record, the spell was never reversed. The tiger eventually went to the closest zoo to live, and the uncle was never seen again. It is about six months before he is given a proper memorial service.

10

Setting Up Home with Uninvited Guests 1994

With several containers shipped, my plan is slowly coming together, and I'm getting settled into my home. My home has three hundred watts of electricity. That means I can burn three, one hundred-watt lightbulbs, or I can use a few forty-watt bulbs and have a fax, a cassette player for music, and a small fridge. The infrastructure of this remote town is so meager that there is not one extra watt of electricity to be had. Only the three hundred watts will be available to me until the government upgrades the infrastructure, whenever that is. I try seducing the men-in-charge by

bribing the corrupt government officials, neighbors, and anyone else I can think of to get additional wattage until I establish that the electricity is so valuable that even the poorest of people will not sell a watt. This means *no* air-conditioning in my two rooms, which means enduring a hot, balmy, humid, tropical environment. This time, my relative wealth can't rescue me from Third World conditions.

The barbed wire atop my walls always offends me, making it appear that I don't trust the local people. However, Atos, Carlton, and Huda insist that it stay, especially as I'm the only white female in a five-hour radius and thus fascinating to the locals. I continue to sleep under a mosquito net, and most nights I simply sweat myself to sleep. Because of limited electricity, I cannot run a pump, leaving me with limited running water. I continue to use a cold mandi for bathing. But at least I have a flushing toilet.

In my kitchen, I have a small two-top gas burner that I use as a stove with a tin box that sits on top creating an oven. I purchase the largest fridge I can find in Semarang; it is all of three and a half feet tall. I produce a small amount of furniture for myself including a four-poster bed, two large oversized Colonial-style couches that sit facing each other, and

a Dutch-style coffee table that sits between the colossal-size sofas. I also produce six mahogany and rattan dining chairs to sit around the two hundred-year-old solid teak Javanese dining table that I find and purchase, along with a traditional antique desk for my office. I also locate a French armoire to use as my closet. I have custom-built candleholders from my brass vendors and bring the extra-large candles from Bali, the ones used for special ceremonies; together, they stand nearly three feet tall.

While living in Bali, I had custom art painted that measures two meters by two meters with jungle scenes of tigers, elephants, giraffes, and monkeys hidden and tucked in the jungle scenes. I had collected some of Bali's most exceptional handicrafts including torches, eight-foot giraffes, large mirrors made from ocean seashells, and huge coconut wood plant stands that measure five feet in height. I take wild orchids from the trees and weave them into pillars at the compound. As I sit alone in silence every night, I admire the basic but charming quarters that I call home.

My home reminds me of Daddy's deer camps in which he and I spent so much time. This, however, is much more appealing than Daddy's camps,

with the collection of furniture and items that I have so scrupulously selected, including the tall candles, torches, and dupa or incense. It all stretches from one end of the house to the other, with vast amounts of tropical flora which I have planted everywhere. The foliage I've planted becomes thick and quickly blankets the brick walls with green color, making my home more serene, lush, and fresh. At night with lamps, candles, torches, and plants, the insects come. The insects bring geckos, bats, and mice. The geckos, bats, and mice bring the local wild cats. I find myself often sitting under the stars in the gardens ducking from the bats one minute and being startled by wild cats the next.

Huda hires Bidjo, an ex-military soldier, as my nighttime security guard. Bidjo comes every evening at sunset, naps on the teak bench in front of my home and leaves every morning at sunrise. He asks nothing of me but an envelope with a small amount of money in it once a month. For that, he vows to protect me with his life. He often brings me lovely fruit from the fruit trees in his village. I learn how blessed he feels being employed by me, and again, it teaches me how to count *my* blessings every day. I continue to learn from these people.

I decide that I don't need domestic help, and that doing the chores will give me something to do in the evenings. I am now ready to start cooking meals for myself, so I go to the local market to get chicken. Yes, rice and chicken would be a good start along with some ka kancung, a local green similar to spinach. As I walk through the local market or pasar, smelling the fish that had been set out and sold during the hot, hot day, I feel a little queasy as my stomach tries to gargle up through my throat. Glad I decided on chicken. In my best bahasa, I ask for *chicken*. To my total dismay, I am handed a live and squirming chicken with its feet tied together, and it is STILL clucking. I decide very quickly that I *do need* domestic help, a *pembantu*, after all.

As I am exiting the market, I run into Carlton, the Englishman. He invites me over for dinner, as he has guests in town and is hosting a dinner party tonight. I've seen pictures of his beautiful Italian wife, Isabella, and ask if she will be there.

Carlton explains that Isabella is currently in Italy, but his friends visiting from Bali have all brought their girlfriends, either of Balinese or Javanese descent. It will be a lovely night of dining with wine, music, and all that stuff. "Yes, I would be delighted to attend!" I

exclaim, all smiles. Ah, civilization, I think, and lucky me for the invite; I swear I'm nearly starving to death.

Entering Carlton's new home, I am utterly fascinated. The structure has been renovated to have new walls, tiled floors, and a lovely thatched roof with ponds and falls. The interior is filled with grand Balinese and Javanese antiques, art, statuaries, relief carvings, etc. It is like walking through a grand Southeast Asian museum, but better yet, quickly at my side is a pembantu inquiring if I prefer red wine or white wine. Lovely music plays throughout the house. Shortly thereafter, homemade appetizers are being passed, most of them recipes from Isabella's grandmother back in Italy. The house, music, food, and wine seem like heaven!

Carlton's guests are several European males visiting from various places, each accompanied by a "local" girl who speaks English well, and they are wise to the ways of the Western man. I am handed something, a little pipe of some sort, but I don't smoke, so I decline. I inquire what's in the pipe. I didn't smell the fragrant cloves of the local tobacco, and so I make the assumption it's an import tobacco.

"Hashish," states one of the visitors.

"Oh really, what's that?" I further inquire. Laughing and in sheer disbelief, he begins to explain to me what hashish is. I was the person in college who studied very hard and worked several jobs, so pot, cannabis, weed, or hashish really never interested me. I had way too much studying on my plate to even pay attention or to bother with it, much less partake. Stunned, but more embarrassed, I stutter that I hadn't understood his accent. Later, I learned that one of the guests visiting Carlton was his "dealer" from Bali bringing his supply of hashish, cocaine, and ecstasy for him and all of his friends. Not participating in the pipe ritual that continues, I delight in the dining, conversation, and sharing of stories.

The altruism of a nice evening that I hadn't enjoyed in over a year made me feel like it was Christmas. I also witnessed that living in the jungle could be made into an exciting and enjoyable colonialist lifestyle. This scene could've been the setting of any African movie I had seen of the early days. I now know more of what I need to do to make this jungle life somewhat gratifying and to truly be able to call it home.

I hire my pembantu, Ningseh, from the Aceh province of West Sumatra. She was widowed and

left with two sons. Ningseh doesn't speak a word of English, doesn't cook Western food but is willing to learn and needs the job badly. I am able to get a reference from one of my workers that she is known to have good character. What more can I really ask for at this point? I can only think how brave she is and give her the job.

Together, we start by making a list of words that would allow us to communicate: cucumber–timun, carrot–wortel, chicken–ayam, rice–nasi, broom–nonexistent; oh, but that thingy of bamboo sticks tied together that I have seen everywhere.

I give Ningseh money to go to the local market to purchase cooking utensils that she knows how to use. It seems she has never before seen the ones that I have acquired. Ningseh also needs to buy cleaning supplies that she's accustomed to using, several of those other "thingys" I've never seen before. We set out learning from each other, starting with creating standards for cooking, cleaning, laundry, and several other things. Ningseh goes to the market early each morning to acquire the ingredients for the meals we will attempt to cook together for that day. While I'm at the factory, she preps the ingredients with care,

along with cleaning the compound and hand-washing my clothes.

One evening, I return home from Semarang after buying supplies for the factory and some groceries from the Gelael Pasar Swalayan, the largest supermarket chain in Indonesia. As we unpack the items, to my surprise, I discover that my new pembantu has never set eyes on any of my purchases ever in her life. It's all new to her! She doesn't know that the cheese goes into the fridge, has no idea what peanut butter is, what is this yellow stuff called butter, and she has never seen a can of tomato sauce, much less what she's supposed to do with this strange thing called a can. Do I cook the can? It seems ages before I start getting lovely and healthy meals like the ones served at Carlton's house. Ningseh's fascination never wanes, similar to the fascination of a child learning new things. It's six months before she is able open a can with a can opener. The first time she answered the telephone, she heard a voice through the handset and was so startled that she threw the phone across the room in fear and began screaming, "There is someone stuck in this box! Help them, help them!" She never becomes discouraged, nor do I. Ningseh

has come a long way, but we still have a long way to go together.

It's the middle of the night, and my phone rings. This isn't so uncommon because I am doing business in the States, accommodating the time zone differences of eleven-to-thirteen hours. The call is from my main customer who lives in Florida. He is elated with the furniture he is receiving, wants more, more, more; but he's concerned about the amount of breakage in the container during transit. I inquire with Huda, Carlton, Atos, and my shipping agent in Semarang, only to learn that my breakage is beyond the norm. Up to two percent is allowed or considered normal, but I am experiencing about four percent. The only element that my factory doesn't do in-house is to *stuff* or pack each container, and in fact neither do the other factories. Once all the furniture is produced, padded with foam, well-wrapped, tied and ready for shipping, a time is set to stuff the container.

Professionals known as "the stuffing team" are called, and each piece of furniture is packed into place, making the contents come together like an elaborate and intricate puzzle. Smaller and lighter items are placed on top of larger and heavier fur-

niture, with legs and smaller pieces woven together tightly and delicately to maximize the use of space while minimizing breakage. I soon determine that we aren't using the most advanced stuffing team. We have been muscled into using the team that works this village, described to me as the "mafia." I learn that this is one of the motivating factors compelling Carlton to relocate his factory to another village. Being muscled into anything just isn't acceptable to me. Too much breakage in my containers is less acceptable. "Huda, fire them! Get me the stuffing team you all tell me about. Cepat, cepat! Immediately," I order.

The new stuffing team moves into place, and another container ships.

I now have a factory driver that I can send to Semarang in my vehicle to search for factory supplies. When this happens, this leaves me without transportation, so Huda arranges for one of the supervisors to take me home on his scooter. The supply list is so long that I don't expect to see the driver or my car until tomorrow. I will be just fine tonight without the four-wheel drive; after all, I have Bidjo, my trusted security guard who will be here in a few hours. I thank the person who brings me home, and off he goes on his scooter.

As soon as I open the door, I hear Ningseh screaming hysterically. I run into the house where she is jumping up and down, crying and screaming incomprehensible words, "Ular, ular! Racun, racun!" Ningseh is frantically pointing to something. My eyes follow her hand to where she is pointing; I, too, am struck by fright. About twenty feet in front of us in the compound is a snake: about six feet long, bright green with a slender body, rearing its head nearly two feet off the ground. It's nervous but so agile that I think it might scale the wall. It displays rapid and frenzied movements, hissing plenty while exposing long front fangs, its head forming a hood and swiveling side to side.

Being a Texas girl, I've seen my share of snakes, but I have never seen one like this. I run to the kitchen counter and grab the Indonesian dictionary and look up the word *poisonous* as quickly as I can, "Racun?!" I inquire.

"Racun, racun!" Ningseh screams back. The words slap me upside the head, shit! "Racun!" Poisonous! I mentally do a quick inventory in my head of the items presently in the house that I can use to kill the snake; there's a small hand shovel for gardening and a frying pan. Nope, neither will work.

I run outside to my neighbor's house. I see home-made gardening tools leaning against the house. I grab one and turn. I see the neighbor looking at me, and she starts to smile. Then she notices I'm stealing her tools. As I look into her face, I can see her thinking, "Great, the white woman has already turned into a maniac." I have no time to explain as I run back into the house allowing her to think I am stealing her tools.

I have to get close to this thrashing serpent. I say a little prayer, exhale a long breath while gathering my nerves and steady myself, and go in for the kill. With the first quick swing, I have the snake's neck pinned underneath the hoe, and the odds of this with its erratic behavior is highly unlikely, but I am lucky. I put all the pressure I can muster onto the snake's neck, praying that the homemade hoe won't break. Once I know the snake is injured and badly hurt, I raise the hoe up over my head and chop down on the snake's neck with all my might, and then again and again and again. An angel had to be with me; the snake is dead, and we are merely shaken. I calm Ningseh, as she is sobbing and trembling in fear. I look around the compound trying to make sense of what has just happened. I infer that the snake must

distraction

live in the trees above and fell into the compound. *Shit, are there more?*

I ask Ningseh to fix dinner for me to eat later so that she can go home early. With the hoe, I carry the snake outside. My neighbor comes over to see what I have. She jumps back with a shriek, and soon, villagers are coming around to see what the excitement is all about. A crowd gathers, but I return to the house. As I walk back into the open area, something catches my eye. I look up on the roof of my sleeping quarters; there is another snake of the same description, slithering rapidly out of control down into the compound. Now, I'm officially horror-struck. Is there a snake nest right above my room and home? Ningseh screams; I then hear pounding on my front door and someone shouting.

I yell, "Ningseh, its Bidjo, let him in!" Bidjo running into the house, having seen the snake outside, grabs the hoe from my hand and immediately pursues the snake. Once the snake is skillfully killed, he looks at me gravely, shaking his head from side to side and mumbling; he and the snake disappear. A large crowd has gathered outside of my home, and Bidjo reappears, looking disturbed. He hunts and inspects the perimeter of the compound, knocks

around in the trees but finds nothing of significance. I send Ningseh home. I'm not sure at this point if I'll see her again.

Feeling unnerved and tense, I wonder how I will calm down for the night. The darkness and the night have come; will these agile, quick, and nasty serpents stalk me again? I want to go to the Ratu Shima to hang out, to get out of this house, but have no vehicle. I pace the house for the next several hours. THERE'S ANOTHER ONE! I see this snake on the roof of my bedroom. But fortunately, it reverses and slithers over the other side of the wall. I run to Bidjo and tell him what I've seen. Another search for the snake is launched, and Bidjo successfully finds and kills it. That is number three and counting. How am I going to sleep tonight? I only have swinging doors on my sleeping quarters. I try to convince myself it is unlikely a snake will crawl into my tall, four-poster bed with a mosquito net but SHIIIT! With my every step in the house, I carry a flashlight and a hoe.

I get ready for bed and try to read myself to sleep. I toss and turn, toss and turn, and toss and turn some more. No way am I going to sleep. I sit up in the middle of the bed on my knees and shine the flashlight around the room, through the net. I want

to get out of bed, but what if a snake is underneath the bed, what if he slithered in during the darkness? I wrap my arms around myself, and tears begin to slide down my cheeks. I soon talk myself back into bravery: I will NOT allow myself to be trapped nor will I be weak. I open the mosquito net and jump as far away from the bed as I can, landing and swiftly turning to shine the light underneath the bed, so far no snakes. I shine the light around the room, inspecting it closely, quickly walking to the lamp to turn it on. "All clear," I exhale.

Again, pacing the house, I hear a knock at the door. It's eleven o'clock at night, so who can this be? I look out through the peephole, and there stands Carlton. I open the door, and Carlton says, "I have been trying to call you, obviously without any luck. I happened to be driving by and saw all the lights on. Your security guard said that you were home."

"Yes, come in, come in. Please come in," I insist. I am breaking all the rules, having a man come into my home while I am there alone, as this is hugely frowned upon in the Muslim religion. But there aren't any rules that prohibit snakes from entering my house, so who cares about the rules at this moment?

"Did you know that your phone is out of order?" asks Carlton.

"No, I didn't," I say as I walk over to the phone/fax to check. "No dial tone." I begin to distractedly ponder, is this a coincidence? Snakes and now no phone? I get Bidjo, and we go outside to check the line. The line has been cut. A new cadence of fear trembles through my body.

"Are you all right? You look upset and even shaken if I might add."

"No, I am not all right." I recap to Carlton the events of the evening. He is flabbergasted, and he has never heard of anything like this in the village. I appeal to Carlton to stay a bit longer, and he agrees, knowing how unsettled I am.

"By the way, Carlton, why have you come by in the first place and at this hour?" I inquire amusingly because I am ecstatic he is here, thinking again there *is* an angel watching over me.

"As I've said, I've been trying to call you. I have something to ask you."

"And what would that be?" I ask, suddenly feeling uncertain.

distraction

"Well, I'm getting married next month, and I'd like for you to be a witness and a guest at my wedding."

"Um…I don't understand, aren't you and Isabella already married?"

"Yes, we are. But I'm going to marry my second wife. I LOVE this country, and I LOVE this religion," he proudly states.

I choke and stutter, "WHAAT? What…do…you…mean, what are you talking about?!"

"The Muslim religion allows for four wives, even five is an option here. I like the idea. I want at least three wives, if not four."

"Uh…umm…really? I didn't think you were Muslim. What does Isabella think of this?"

"I'm not Muslim, but when in Rome, you know," he smiles and shrugs. "Well, I must admit. Isabella isn't totally buying into it. She's in Bali right now. After I approached her with my plan, she refused to return to Jepara. But she *will* come around. By Muslim law, I need her approval for the second marriage. She actually hasn't spent much time here anyway."

"Do you actually think she is going to give you her approval? Do you *really* expect her to, Carlton?"

"Of course I expect her to. But I've accepted that if she doesn't, I will just find another new wife or two, and I will find wives who appreciate me. She doesn't particularly like Jepara."

"I cannot fathom a Western woman approving. I would find it…appalling myself. I've heard nothing but lovely things about Isabella. Are you willing to really lose her for these shenanigans…now? What about later, when you are tired of these games, you will have *forced* her away?"

"No worries, mate, I'll be fine," he says as he shrugs again.

You JERK, I'm thinking. "So you've already met someone," I state. "And already engaged?"

He smiles lovingly, or is it smugly? "Yes, her name is Saniyati. We have been dating for about six months. She is beautiful and lovely and cherishes me. We will have a large, traditional Javanese wedding. All of her family and friends will attend and so will mine from Bali, and my mom and brother from England."

"Why do you want me to be the witness at your wedding? I don't know the bride, and I do not support you on this either, Carlton. I think you are rather…mad."

"Yes, I understand; however, I would like you to reconsider. I would like someone who is…honorable…respected…like you, as our witness, for Saniyati's sake. She deserves that, and she is rather shy around all of my male friends."

"I can understand that and even sympathize with her. But, Carlton, I cannot accept this invitation." *Not under any circumstance*, I'm thinking. "I cannot accept it, *but* it is *your* prerogative to believe or choose whatever you care to. That's the best I can offer here, acceptance."

It's now after two o'clock in the morning. I tell Carlton that my nerves are now settled and thank him for staying a while longer and chatting with me. No more snakes and no more incidents for hours now. I do sleep, but very lightly.

I awaken to the "call of prayers" as "Allahu Akbar…Allahu Akbar…" echoes from the nearby mosques. This morning, I find these prayers particularly comforting as the words mean, "Allah is the greatest or God is the greatest."

It's just after sunrise, and there's a loud knock at the door. Now who ? It's Huda. "What are you doing here?" I ask.

"Bidjo found me immediately after prayers this morning. We have a problem. The snakes in your home; these snakes aren't indigenous to the area. There is only one source for this type of snake around here."

"WWWhat? WWWhere?" I ask, feeling repulsed.

"These snakes came from a snake man, a special black magic shaman. The snake is a green mamba. It is very venomous, capable of killing rapidly with a single bite."

As this information sinks in. I walk to the closest chair, collapse into it and sit petrified starring at Huda, "But…Who? Why?"

"We have to find that out, but Bidjo and I have an idea. I'll make some inquiries. What time do you want me to send a scooter for you?"

"Uh, make it at eight I guess."

Upon my arrival at the factory, Huda isn't around. I find my concentration shattered, and my thoughts discombobulated. My head is all over the place; my Bahasa seems nonexistent. It's hours before Huda finally arrives back at the factory. I notice he appears a little relieved versus how he had been at my home earlier this morning.

"Did you learn anything?" I ask anxiously.

As he shakes his head yes, he says, "The snakes were ordered by the mafia stuffing team."

With this new intelligence, I find myself speechless. I have a thousand questions racing through my mind, which one do I start with? "Really! You've got to be kidding me!" are the most intelligible, authoritative words that I can sputter from my lips as I incredulously gawk at Huda with eyes wide open and chin fully dropped.

"I have confirmed it with the black magic shaman that was hired to release the green mambas at your home. He did it."

Again, the million questions fluttering through my mind as my gawking continues, with my eyes and mouth still wide open. "He admitted to it?" I manage to ask.

Huda shakes his head yes again.

"Isn't that against the law? Can we call the police on them...him...them?"

Now Huda stares at me with *his* eyes wide open and chin fully dropped, "Uhh...uhh," then he shakes his head no. "I don't think there are really any laws against black magic."

As it sinks in that I am really having this bizarre conversation, I ask, "So what do *you* suggest we do in light of this information?"

"We hire the stuffing team back immediately," Huda states strongly.

"NO! Absolutely NOT!"

"Really? But, Ms. Satrece, we don't have a choice. They are serious. Their mafia beliefs have them thinking that they are entitled to all the business in this village. Also, *you*, *a woman*, fired them. They must save face."

Ahhhhhh, that face-saving thing. It's not the first time I've experienced it, nor will it be the last. But green mambas or not, they're not forcing my usage of them if they can't do the job or guarantee their work. "There must be an agreement we can come to."

I notice the thought had never crossed Huda's mind; it was an automatic surrender to him as well as to the others who knew of the incident. "Really? You think? Like what?"

"Can we request a meeting with them and try to 'nego' a solution to this problem?" "Nego" or nee-go or negotiating is a widely and frequently used word throughout the Indonesian archipelago. Very few

Indonesians—Javanese, Balinese or Sumatrans—can resist a nego, if for no other reason than curiosity.

As Huda thinks about it, he then says, "Yeah? Yeah, we can give that a try."

Guess who is waiting for my arrival on the outside entrance of the factory the next morning? The entire mafia group is just sitting patiently, awaiting my arrival.

Allowing them to save face, I greet them with a smile and handshakes like nothing ever happened.

I put my things away and join them along with Huda, all casually sitting around the front entrance porch area. Huda has bought a case of bottled sweet tea, Sosro teh, always consumed at room temperature, and a bag of local snacks for the occasion. I join in the traditional practice of snacks and warm tea and participate in all the small talk and gossip. Indonesians love to gossip as much as they like to nego. Me being the Westerner and only having so much patience, I break the ice, asking them what we should do about our little misunderstanding. Without any hesitation, the appointed spokesperson speaks back with a smile and a kind soft voice, "It is very easy; hire us back."

I give them a kind, gentle laugh, and I tell them that this does settle their problem, but not mine. I reiterate that the breakage in my containers is double that of industry standards, and that is not acceptable. I ask how they are going to do a better job stuffing my containers and what guarantees they are going to give.

This sparks a major conversation among themselves; I didn't think it would ever end. At last, they finally inform me there is nothing they can do better or different, that this is how they stuff. I give them credit for being honest, amazingly enough. They send green mambas after me but have honor in their word. I explain to them that if they can't do the job properly, I will eventually get a bad reputation and go bankrupt. I tell them, "I cannot pay you to make me bankrupt. What would you do if you were in my situation?" Again, they launch into another extensive debate amongst themselves. I take Huda to the side and offer some ideas and options and ask him to establish himself as the person to nego on our behalf. I leave to let him do what he does best. I excuse myself and tell them I will be inside and available if they need me.

distraction

Hours pass. Huda sends for more snacks and bottled tea. Huda updates me every several hours, but sees no progress. They have rejected every idea and option I had offered. Huda and I talk among ourselves again, brainstorming ideas for him to propose. An hour before closing, I join the group on the front porch for an update. Six hours of nego, and we are right where we started. They have a reputation and cannot make any exceptions, period. Huda is extremely worried about green mambas visiting me again and strongly suggests that I pay them their normal fee for each container but also hire the avant-garde stuffing team to do the actual work. I then realize their fee isn't too much money and at last agree to Huda's proposition. They get *their* money, I get *my* stuffing team and a promise of no more green mambas, but I feel disgust to my bones. After I concede, they quickly agree to turn their head on twenty percent of my containers to show good faith but will collect normal fees on the rest. We paid the mafia stuffing team for years. They were paid as long as we remained in Ngabul Village, but I was never visited by the green mambas again.

The next week, I am off to Singapore for a visa run. A well-needed escape.

11

Ron Arrives in Indonesia
June 2008

"A re you here in Southeast Asia?"

"Yes, I arrived a few hours ago. I just walked into my room."

"Where are you exactly?"

"Exactly, huh?" Ron chuckles. "Exactly, I'm in Jakarta, I'm at the Shangri-La Hotel, our company's preferred hotel in Jakarta."

"Well, may I be the first to welcome you to Indonesia?"

"Yes, I would like that. Thank you. That brings a smile to my face. Like you said, it is a *long* trip here. I had forgotten how long of a trip it is."

distraction

I'm always filled with exhilaration landing any place in Southeast Asia; so much so, I feel a sense of excitement and thrill for Ron. Feeling a true connection, I inquire about the details of his trip. Ron flew Continental Airlines from Houston to LA, then boarded Singapore Airlines to Singapore and onward to Jakarta.

Ron's meetings include Jakarta for several days, then returning to Singapore for two more days of meetings and will come back to Jakarta for one night before transiting to Balikpapan, East Kalimantan for another day of business. Upon returning from Kalimantan, his vacation will begin.

It genuinely stimulates me that Ron is significantly successful enough to have business in and out of Jakarta, Singapore and throughout Indonesia. Reality smacks me for the first time that Ron is actually here in Indonesia—in Jakarta—and his trip is motivated by his desire to see me again. This partially excites me yet distresses me considerably. I have really savored our conversations together, whether it had been by text, e-mail, or phone. But on the contrary, he utterly confuses the hell out of me too! The voice on the other end of the phone has become familiar, perceptive, and gratifying. He has become a

friend over the last two months bringing smiles and humor amid tough situations. A friend is one thing, but a romance? Not likely. I must concede to myself, I'm not sure I even remember exactly what he looks like. This whole enchilada of Ron pressing to see and meet me again is mind-boggling. What doesn't he get? I *will not* abandon my people, my business, nor my life to return to the States to be someone's significant other. And of course, he wouldn't be terminating his employment to move to the jungle to help the unfortunate, make furniture, and to live a life of adventure. What's the use?

Ron asks, "What's all the noise in the background? Normally when we talk, I hear waterfalls, and it always sounds so peaceful."

"Normally when we talk, I'm at home. I am at the factory now. You hear compressors and generators, sanding machines, screw and nail guns, etc., just to name a few. It's always very noisy here, and in the office, I have very little privacy."

Ron again tries to imagine this mysterious creature, someone as exquisite as she, in a Third World factory in the jungle. He just can't absorb it. How is this? Why is it?

distraction

"How is everything going for you now? Is it getting any better?"

"No, not really. My staff and I put out one fire and another one erupts. My brother and I just recently returned from Bali to another round of issues to resolve."

"I am pleased to hear that you returned safely. Did you and your brother have an enjoyable time?"

"Yes, of course! Who doesn't enjoy Bali? I mostly hung out on the beach and kick-started my tan. I swam a lot in the ocean and enjoyed some well-needed relaxation. This allowed my brother to do whatever he fancied. Uh, Ron, can we continue this conversation a little later? I apologize, but something here seems to need my immediate attention."

"I understand. May I call you again tonight? Now that I am here in country, I can't imagine not speaking with you more often."

"Yes, that will be fine," Satrece says as she hangs up her cell phone.

Sholikin, the upholstery manager who had been waiting for me, exclaims, "Ms., the fabric and foam reps are here. The import products that we normally purchase for our upholstery products are no longer available with the weak rupiah as they are now

too expensive for them to carry. They have brought samples similar to what we have been using, so will you please look at them and see if something is acceptable?

Huda, who is also waiting close by, calls out to me, "Ms., the Impra rep for our finishing products is here too with the same problem. Will you come meet with us when you finish with Sholikin?"

"Hi, so it's you again, huh?" Satrece says teasingly into the phone later that night.

"Yes, it is. Did you get your problems sorted out at the factory?"

"No, not really. It's all ongoing for now. Enough of that. What did you do the rest of the day?"

"I made contact with my local office here in Jakarta, confirmed my meetings for tomorrow and got myself organized."

"Did you get any rest after your long trip?"

"No, I'm far too excited to rest. Have you given any more thought on where you would like to travel when we meet up?"

"No, not really."

"Hmmm…why is that?"

"Do you really expect me to run off with a man I've only met one time, who I hardly know? Really? I just truly can't conceive it; I'm having a hard time with this. I'm sorry."

"Well, I can understand your point of view. Actually, it pleases me immensely that you are reluctant to consider it," Ron says gently and continues, "but consider this: if we want to indeed get to know each other better, it will take more than one evening with dinner. Having come all this distance, I won't leave until my business is completely finished. I won't have a *business* reason to return to Asia anytime in the near future." Suddenly, Ron adds, "And of course, you know you will have your own room and your privacy no matter where we choose to go."

"Well, no, I didn't know that. I mean, I didn't know what your expectations were of me."

"Now that offends me. You certainly can't imagine I expect more from you, do you?"

"Uuh, it's never been mentioned, nor clarified. And yes, from most men that I've met, that is exactly what they would expect."

"I'm so sorry for being vague; I should have been clearer. No wonder you have been so noncommittal and reserved and especially with the other

challenges you are facing. But I assure you that I don't expect anything of you that would make you the slightest bit uncomfortable."

I instinctively let out a long, deep exhale. For the first time, I don't feel I am being pressured into doing something I don't want to do. As I contemplate all that has just been said, with expectations clarified, I can undeniably understand Ron's point of view. Then I notice my long silence while sifting through my thoughts and recognize that Ron is giving me time to assimilate it all. He is a unique man.

"Vietnam."

"Vietnam? What about Vietnam?"

"That's the only place in Southeast Asia that I have never been. All other places, I already know like the back of my hand and consider them my playground. Vietnam would be the next place I would choose to travel."

"Unbelievable, that is exactly where I was thinking! Based on what you've told me about your travels, that's the only place in the region I can think of that might be a first-time visit for both you and me. Perfect! So we will meet in Jakarta for a date, and if all goes well, we're off to Vietnam?" Ron asks lightheartedly.

Laughingly, "Assuming you pass the first date, yes, we are off to Vietnam. Wow! I can't believe it. I am actually considering going off with a man that I've just met. But, Ron, there is something you should know about me."

"What's that, Satrece?"

"If you *don't* pass the first date, I *will* be on the next flight home."

Ron laughs. "I have no doubt about that, but how could you not absolutely adore me?"

I remember it was his confidence that I found so attractive the first time I laid eyes on him—and his smile, which I can *hear* all the time.

I walk out of my bedroom, and David, my brother, gives me the third degree. "Where have you been?" He puffs his cigar holding it in one hand and a Bintang beer in the other.

He's four years my senior and a big ole country boy. He's euphoric to be here in Indonesia. David is eager to involve himself in my life, desiring to live here and work in my factory. He would sever his right arm for me, but it is David who always needs help. He still grieves for not having other family or me close by. My blazing new trails in the jungle leaving

him behind in America nearly crushed him. David is still seeking his own northern compass point.

"On the phone," I answer.

"Talking to *that* same guy again?"

"Yes," Satrece laughs. "*That* same and only guy."

"What's that all about? That ain't like you, I've never known you to be interested in guys...period."

"True," Satrece says, as she contemplates her brother's words. "He has just invited me to go to Vietnam with him. He's a little different than other men. He seems successful, very well-travelled, worldly, wise, and I don't know. There is just something about him. I really enjoy talking to him. He seems to actually understand me and accept me and still wants to get to know me more."

"No shit, Sherlock! Every man wants to get to know you better or wants something from you or even ends up stalking you."

"Oh, don't remind me of the past. Please."

"Well, are you going away with him? I'm happy to stay here and watch the factory for you. I can call you if more problems arise or at least keep you informed about how things are going."

"Yes, I guess...I've just accepted. However, you're aware of all the issues going on at the moment.

distraction

I really shouldn't be leaving again. There are so many people counting on me, and this isn't the time for me to be gallivanting across the globe nor is it the time for a man to distract me."

"Go. I have you covered on this. Enjoy yourself," David insists.

This is the opportunity David has been looking for to wiggle himself into the operations of the factory. Well, more power to him if he can, but he'll have to earn it.

The next morning, Satrece is greeted by Huda the moment she walks into the factory. Huda's face is very serious and grim. "Pagi Huda, apa kabar? Bagaimana semua?" Satrece greets him good morning and asks how he's doing, and how everything is, while searching the expression on his face. Huda journeyed into Semarang the day prior to meet with the Government of Agriculture, which owns and manages the building and grounds we presently operate from. It is a beautiful compound built in 1932 by Dutch settlers who cultivated the local rice fields. It survived World War I and World War II and is surrounded by beautiful, large green rice fields with a stream running through the middle. A continuous gentle breeze passes through the compound,

spawning peaceful and positive energy. By now, the factory has been in this compound for ten years. It's large and offers numerous warehouses with room to grow. I have expanded the factory several times. I've tried time and time again to purchase the buildings and land, but being owned by the Agriculture Department, it cannot be sold. Through the years, I've gained trust and respect for the government officials managing the property. They like leasing the property and have assured me that this is a win-win scenario for both of us. I feel secure in their commitment. In the ten years we have been doing business together, they have never broken a promise, always keeping their word.

Huda tells me that all of the original officials have been replaced with new people. He has no idea what has happened to the original contacts, but they are gone. This news brings me great apprehension and concern. Huda proceeds to update me with the prior day's events and tells me how the new team of government officials left him waiting for a very long time. When they finally did meet with Huda, their greetings were not the usual and customary hospitable chatter of gossip and recent events. The new people went directly into business, getting right to

the point. Huda explains they made a strong case. In light of the worldwide financial crisis, local governments need to rapidly respond to inflationary pressures stemming from the dual food and energy crisis. The financial, monetary and fiscal policies will be changing, and it is starting here and now.

"So, what does this mean to us?" I ask Huda the same questions he asked the officials. It means a 400 percent increase in the lease price of our factory.

Outrage fills my entire body. "Are they insane? Nobody raises prices 400 percent! Surely they're just bluffing, and this is the beginning of their 'nego.'"

Huda shakes his head. "I don't think so, Ms. Satrece...I think they're serious."

We both sit and stare into space thinking about the repercussions for us. "Now what? What do we do?" asks Huda.

"There's no way they can really expect an increase that big. Do you think they're trying to end this contract because they have other plans for this building?" Satrece mumbles.

"No, I don't. There are enough other problems in the country. I don't see the government developing projects in times like this. I asked the same question, and they assured me not."

Satrece

"Well, for now, let's just wait for a bit and allow them to think that we're not interested. Say some prayers, we are going to need them."

We sit in silence a while longer, deep in thought. "That's not our only problem either, Ms. Satrece."

"What? What else is going on?"

"In the newspaper today, it says that the tax department will be auditing all expatriate-owned factories for the same fiscal reasons we discussed, and they will be starting the audits immediately."

"Ahhhh…Gjeeshk!" Taxes for the factory are the one thing that I don't get involved in on a local level, and this is a responsibility that I leave entirely to Huda and Susi, our accountant. From what I know, it's common custom to have two sets of financial records, a real set of books and a tax set of books. In the early years when I learned of this practice and of our second set of books, I erupted in a dissertation contending that defrauding the tax department cannot and will not be tolerated. I explained about our good ole IRS and what would happen to me if I were to defraud them. My team responded by simply stating that they are not reporting to the IRS; they are reporting to their local Indonesian tax authorities, and this is the way it's done here. My team listened to

me out of respect, but as I continued to receive blank stares, I realized their decision was made. I knew my arguments were falling on deaf ears and decided the less I knew on this topic, the better. Special note: through the years, I took pride in the taxes I paid or didn't pay, as I liked doing business in Indonesia.

"I will call my sources to see what I can learn about this, and you do the same, please," Satrece says to Huda.

"I have already called our tax consultant. He said that it is a problem. It's a problem for us, for him, and for every other factory that will be audited," Huda sighs.

Later in the afternoon, Ron calls, "After I finished my meetings today, I was able to accomplish a lot for us."

"Oh really? Accomplish what for us?"

"Planning our trip to Vietnam."

"Oh yes, of course, the trip to Vietnam."

"I have spoken to my colleagues that work and frequently travel to the area and have compiled a list of recommendations of things for us to do and see and the best hotels and places to eat. This is going to be an awesome trip. By the way, is there anything

in particular that you're interested in seeing or doing while there?"

"Uh, no. I haven't done any research on the area, and I'm not particularly knowledgeable on Vietnam. I always buy a travel book before I go to a new country and read up on it…but …"

"If you don't mind, I'm happy to plan this for us. I would enjoy it."

"Yes, good. Thanks. It isn't often that people do things for me."

"Uhh, there is one little detail that you might or might not know," continues Ron.

"What's that?" Satrece asks.

"We need visas. I know of a service here that will expedite them for us, and we will be able to get them in about a week. That is, if we have them rushed, and everything goes as planned. So I guess that means…uh…you will need to send me your… uh passport …"

"Send my passport through an Indonesian courier and send it to you?! Ahhhh…I'd forgotten about the visa. My passport to you? Via courier? Are you sure we can't get them on arrival?"

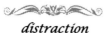

"I'm certain. I understand about sending your passport through a local courier…but there must be some service you trust."

"Gjeeshk. I guess…there's one …that's been continuously dependable. I'll get it out tomorrow. Where do you want me to send it? Won't you be leaving for Singapore shortly?"

"Send it to the Shangri-La Hotel, to my attention. I will see to it that they hold it for me. Don't worry, I will protect your passport with my life," Ron says laughingly and assuredly.

Sending my passport to a man I barely know, to a hotel address for which he is not even at, and hoping all of this goes according to plan seems simply outrageous and nuts to me, Satrece is thinking.

"Is everything okay? You don't quite sound yourself this afternoon."

"It's just work, the same old things," answers Satrece.

"I have a dinner meeting tonight, how late are you usually up? I'd like to talk with you later, if I can," Ron inquires.

"Text me, and if I'm still awake, I'll let you know. With my brother here and all these problems, I'm not sleeping much these days."

"How did your dinner meeting go?" Satrece inquires.

"Great. I had forgotten how much I enjoy it here in Indonesia. It seems I have a legacy here; there're still people in Indonesia that I knew when I worked here and others that know or have heard of me. People are telling me stories of myself that happened over fifteen years ago."

"Wow, I'm impressed, that's neat. Cool, well done."

"You know what else is neat?"

"No, what's that?"

"The time is ticking down, and it won't be too long until I get to see you again. I am really getting excited."

Satrece cuts him off, "Ron, help me with something, I really don't understand."

"Why? What is it?"

"You live in Texas. Texas is known for its beautiful women. Why are you coming halfway around the world to see *me*? Why are you putting yourself and me through this? Why not just date one of those beautiful women that are already living in Texas?" Satrece asks with total sincerity.

Ron bursts into laughter. "Yes, you're exactly correct. Texas *is* full of beautiful women and don't you ever forget, you are one of those beautiful women, and *you* are from Texas! But you're interesting, independent, well-travelled, gracious, and successful too! There's no competition." Ron continues to laugh.

"Oh, for heaven's sake. You are a little bit nutty, aren't you?" Satrece says with exasperation.

"I still see your beauty and elegance when I close my eyes," Ron says with passion.

"My elegance? HA! Boy, are you in for a surprise and disappointment! When we met in the airport that was the Stateside version of me you saw. Here, I wear a ponytail every day, walk around in safari hiking boots, wearing only a little mascara and lip gloss, and khaki shorts or a khaki skirt. There's *nothing* elegant about that."

"Oh, that's okay. I like that look too."

"From what I remember, you strike me more as the designer type of guy with a tendency of being well-polished," Satrece smirks.

"You forgot that I lived in Indonesia for four years and worked in West Africa for another six," chides Ron.

"Um hmm. That's the past. I'm not buying it. I'll send you some pictures tonight before I go to bed, of the Indonesian version of Ms. Satrece. We'll see if you are still interested."

"Please do," Ron smiles.

The next morning, my cell phone rings as soon as I walk into the factory.

"Now you've gone and done it!" Ron exclaims.

"What have I done?" I ask defensively.

"I looked at the pictures you e-mailed me. Now I've really fallen for you! You have that side of you as well? I thought it was just glitz, glamour, and a perfectly manicured person, but you have that real adventurous side too. A bit of a tomboy, are you?"

"If you *only knew!*" Satrece exclaims.

"That's exactly what I am trying to do, get to know you better. By the way, where were these pictures taken?"

"In the Golden Triangle. The triangle being northern Thailand, Myanmar, and Laos. I recently did a guided elephant and river safari. My elephant's name is Hundai, that photo is in Thailand. The one with me meditating in front of the giant golden

Buddha is in Myanmar, and the other photo is me on the Mekong River working my way to Laos."

"See, that's what I mean! This isn't a conversation I'd be having with a woman living in Texas. Most women living in Texas can't imagine the places my work takes me, and they certainly wouldn't have the knowledge that you do and wouldn't be riding elephants in Thailand!" Ron snickers.

"So you are okay with the safari look I sport most of the time?"

"Not only am I okay with it, I adore it!"

"We'll see. Where are the places that you've travelled?" asks Satrece.

"Well, my last international assignment was managing all of West Africa, and I have travelled most of Europe and Russia, Northern Africa and the Middle East, most of Southeast Asia, Australia, New Zealand, and China. And of course living in Indonesia for four years."

"Wow. You HAVE covered a lot of ground. Sounds like even more than me."

"Truly, I've worked and traveled all parts of the globe; I think fifty-three countries at this point, but I've yet to set foot in South America or Antarctica," Ron says.

Satrece offers, "I just love travelling. I love learning new cultures, seeing new places and experiencing everything that I can. There are still so many places that I want to see."

"Yes, I love travelling too. But many of the places I have been, you wouldn't enjoy…like Nigeria."

"I look forward to hearing more about some of those places."

Laughingly, Ron asks, "Would you like to hear something humorous?"

"Sure."

"When I repatriated to the U.S. after living in Indonesia, most people asked me if I had learned to speak the language, my answer was always the same, 'Yes, of course, but it will most likely never be of any use to me. I will *never* use it again unless for some reason I go there on business.' Suddenly, for some reason, I love this language!"

That evening as I sit at the head of my antique dining table, accompanied by David, Ningseh serves a delectable meal of tenggiri fish cooked in the savory and delicate local spices of Sumatra. The birds are plentiful and singing the enchanting evening lullabies while the kitties play close by stalking the lizards. I can't help but admire how my home is so tranquil,

and with improvements of running water, sufficient electricity and air-conditioning in two rooms, I still dine in the open pavilion with candles, fountains, and of course the tropical flora. But the one thing that isn't so tranquil is the sound of my brother droning on with his endless diatribe of chatter. I can't even hear myself think.

"Sis, what's on your mind tonight? Are you listening to me at all?" David asks.

"Oh…no…David, I'm probably not, I'm sorry. Some new things have happened today that I need to think through…and I just don't see a solution."

"What has happened now?"

"I received a phone call today from a prospect of mine, Roger from Furniture Choices. Roger is changing his schedule to visit my factory at a much earlier date. Assuming he can change his airline tickets, and he assures me he can, he will be here next week to bring me his drawings for the creation of his entire new line of furniture. It's an awesome opportunity."

"Well, that's fantastic news! What's there to think about?" David says with excitement.

"I'm supposed to be in Vietnam getting to know Ron better. Re-mem-ber?!"

"Yes, but, sis, this is a great opportunity. You've told me about this project and how it would secure your business through this crisis."

"Yes, that's correct. Everything you say."

"So I guess Vietnam will have to wait until later. Right?"

"Yeah, I guess Vietnam will have to wait...Ron will have to wait," Satrece sighs.

The phone rings. "I suppose that's Ron? Are you going to tell him now?" asks David.

"I don't know ..." Satrece says with her spirit withering.

"Well, hi there! How is the gorgeous and sensational Satrece doing tonight?"

"Umm...great. You sound like you've had *another* awesome day," Satrece forces.

"Yes, I have...but a challenging one. I now clearly see all of the issues this country is facing, and being in and about, it is rather daunting. But that's just part of the job," Ron quips.

"Yes, I guess ..." Satrece mumbles.

"I was just thinking...I'm off to Singapore shortly, what should I get us in Duty Free for our trip? As you had warned, alcohol is *very* expensive and very difficult to get here at the moment. Are

distraction

Cosmopolitans and red wine still the drink of choice, as you shared with me earlier?"

"Yes, it is very expensive and difficult and has been for at least a year now. And yes, a Cosmo is my favorite drink by far, followed by a nice red wine. Oh, and champagne, of course," Satrece adds with her voice finally lifting from the somberness it had carried earlier. He seems to be on top of the world. Why don't I feel that way? I realize with my people feeling such despair; I am clouded in despair as well. My people and I stand together.

Ron and I continue our light-hearted banter, and I decide not to tell Ron, just yet, that I will most likely not join him in Vietnam. I decide to ensure Roger's visit to my factory is firm first. I learn from Ron that he prefers dirty martinis and enjoys both red and white wine. I can hear the passion in his voice about his experiences in Indonesia, past and present. He is so easy to talk with, fun too, but he still hasn't told me that much about his work.

The next morning as I drive to the factory, dread fills my entire body. We, the business, are facing so many problems. I might be audited and possibly be out of a factory; can my business survive? And Furniture Choice's business plan is extremely

169

aggressive; can I meet their production schedules now with all of our challenges? Maybe they'll be open to slowing down their earlier demands, as business can't be growing at the same rapid pace in this economic downfall as it was earlier this year. I also know in my heart of hearts, this isn't the time for me to be leaving the business for personal pleasure. Maybe it's time I admit that I can't go away with Ron. I've got to be smart about my business, about everything; no room for error.

12

Life Goes On in Jepara
1994–1996

*T*he monsoon season comes, and the monsoon season goes. We have two seasons here: the hot season and the rainy season. Once you've experienced the latter, you'll never forget it. The peak of the monsoons is from December through February. It's a period when your home and factory leak profusely no matter how determined you are to prevent it. It's a time when the monsoons are so extreme, rain leaks through the roof and onto your face at night, and all you can do is finally accept it. When your newly washed clothes never dry, you eventually become comfortable wearing damp clothes. It's a time when your sheets and towels have

never smelled so badly, when rats and mice appear from everywhere in efforts not to drown, and you actually pity them. When the electricity is off more than it's on, and I yearn for my measly 300 watts. My evening pastime becomes watching the rats and mice get stuck in the flypaper. And then the cats chase the rats and mice, and while the rats and mice are stuck in the flypaper, the cats get caught in the flypaper too. Then I must chase the cats that are stuck in the flypaper to rescue them. I toss the rumpled flypaper outside in the bin, which is a large deep hole dug into the earth for trash. Soon after, I hear the chickens in the flypaper. I continue to get laughs from the most unlikely events.

I often drive to the factory through the raging floods; no worries, I have the vehicle for it. Most every day, there's a flood and/or a road washed out, producing another detour. Thank goodness I'm a Texas girl, and actually enjoy such challenges. Arriving at the factory, the first thing I do is scour the entire premise for leaks to determine the damage to the materials and furniture. This continues to challenge my patience. My workers seem to turn their eyes the other way, overlooking the leaks. They

distraction

accept it, it's just life here. This is one issue where I can't accept their acceptance. Gjeeshk!

When you begin seeing sleeping mattresses being aired and dried outside, you know that the monsoon season is nearly over. Ningseh and I discuss the maintenance that needs to be done to my home when the rainy season is finished and what to do with the mold and mildew that have taken up residence with us.

Quickly, Ningseh says that she can get someone from her village to come and help us for a few days. Good idea. Ningseh comes to work the next morning with a person in tow. His name is Rifan. Rifan immediately gets to work scrubbing all the mold and mildew from the house and evaluates the other projects needed after the torrential rains. He works hard and has a bright, kind smile. A week turns into a few weeks, a few weeks turn into a month, which turns into more months. The three of us continue to find work and projects for Rifan, including washing my vehicle nearly every day.

I hire Susi into my office staff, as my accountant, having a degree in "Ekonomi Akuntansi." Susi graduated from a prestigious university in Malang, and her uncle is a well-respected government official.

I'm told that her character is solid based on the reputation of her uncle. I have no choice but to have *faith* in the guidance given to me, as she will be handling my money. Let's hope she lives up to her reputation.

Until now, the factory works Saturday through Thursday, as in most Muslim countries, with Friday being the holy day for prayer. Luckily for me, I'm approached by a contingent of workers requesting that we move the workweek to Monday through Saturday. When I inquire why, I'm told that if an event such as a band or a sports match comes to town, they come on Saturday evening or Sunday. It's requested that we change our hours on Friday to accommodate prayers. Jakarta, the capital, made this change a while ago. Heck yeah, I'm in!

Susi now handles payroll for the workers. On payday, now moved to Friday, I go to the bank with a large briefcase and fill it with money in all denominations. Susi sits all afternoon counting the correct denominations of bills for each worker's pay, stapling the bills into envelopes inscribed with each employee's name.

She organizes all the vendors and sets guidelines for them to get paid in similar fashion.

Susi also better organizes my bookkeeping system, so by now, I feel like I'm gaining control and professionalism in my company. This leaves me more time for improving and expanding the factory, more time for designing and marketing new furniture models.

I have figured out that with the amount of workers I have, if one wants to ship a high-quality container of furniture a month, you must finance and have three in progress. To simplify it, one month for the raw furniture to be made, one month for the curing of the wood and finishing including sanding, upholstery, brass and glass installation, etc., and one month for the container to be in transit on the ocean. Then when you want to send two containers a month, you must have six in progress and so on. I ran out of my savings and cash long ago but insist on continuing aid we're providing to the people of the villages, along with sustaining the growth of my business, with financing through my credit cards for over a year now. I'm now carrying $40,000 in credit card debt. With Susi hired, I have more time to focus on the business, hopefully chiseling this amount down.

I've actually become friends with my upholstery manager, Sholikin. He showed up in the factory on

week two and just started working. He never asked for a job, he never asked for a salary, he just started working on his creations. Before long, chaise lounges, grandfather chairs, and love seats were some of our best handiworks. I realize Sholikin is wise in many ways; he proves that he is worthy of the job, and as a manager, he is also up for any challenge. I eventually hire Sholikin as staff. He invites me to his home to meet his mother and father, his wife and new baby. Suddenly, I'm part of the family. Sholikin has a unique story to share with me each day while I check on our next upholstery creations. This challenges me to learn Bahasa better; I want to understand his stories and his unique perspective on things. It was Sholikin that had recommended Ningseh to work in my home.

"So you hired Ningseh's husband to work at your home too?" Sholikin inquires.

"No. Ningseh brought in someone from her village to help us out for a while. He's a very good worker; we're keeping him busy."

"Really? But not Ningseh's husband?"

"No. Her husband died, didn't he?"

"What's the new worker's name?"

"Rifan. Do you know him, Sholikin?"

Sholikin smiles. "I know Rifan, Ningseh's husband. That's the only Rifan I know in our village."

"Rifan is Ningseh's husband? Why didn't they just tell me? He's much younger…Her husband didn't die?" I ask, profoundly confused.

"Yes, she lost her husband. She decided she wanted to come to Java to find work and so did Rifan. They thought being married would make their journey and finding work easier, so they married."

"Does anyone else know this, or is it a secret?"

"Yes, others know. It's no secret."

"Why am I the last one to know?"

"Satrece, the white man…uh…or white woman is always the last to know. Important lesson you should learn." So Confucius says?

Okay, important lesson learned. This is only one of many lessons I learn from Sholikin.

I spent Christmas in the States with my boyfriend and his elderly parents. He proposed marriage early one morning, and before it sank in, or I answered, he'd told his mother, and a wedding was being planned by 9:00 that morning. I really adored his parents; his father was an ex-congressman, and his mother was angelic, and she accepted me imme-

diately, the family that I so wanted. Within four days, we were married in Newport, Rhode Island.

He had been a successful owner of an infamous bar and restaurant, and he was well-liked and adored when we met. He told me upfront that he was an alcoholic but was now sober; I truly didn't know what that meant. He was honest with me and gave a full explanation of the disease and his past behaviors. I asked him how long he had been sober. "Seven years," he replied.

"Do you ever plan in partaking again?" I asked.

He replied, "Absolutely not, and if I ever do, RUN."

That was good enough for me. The grief from my father's death still weighed so heavily on me; I just wanted someone to love. But within two months of living full-time in Jepara, his sobriety was lost. It didn't take him long to find Carlton's drug dealer either. I should have *run* as he advised, but instead, I hung in there, and regret set in. He was on his best behavior before we married; however, I soon got to see his true self. I tried for years to help him, but he nearly destroyed me mentally and emotionally before I could free myself from him.

It was during my time with him that I surrendered my innocence. I learned the world doesn't exist with most people who are all good—most people have shades of gray or even black. There are broken people, people who enjoy hurting others to lessen their own pain, people who know the difference between right and wrong but just don't care, and people who punish themselves hoping to include you in their suffering. It was my first exposure to loud, abusive words, and I learned firsthand what that can do to one's soul. I learned that dignity, loyalty, and truth aren't the laws of human nature; some are not capable of learning such things. But as Forrest Gump would say, "That's all I have to say about that."

Carlton phones to invite me to another dinner party. He and Saniyati are entertaining potential candidates that may move here to Jepara and work for him. Carlton would like these candidates to meet other expats in the area. I'm excited about the prospects of new expats coming and to get out and socialize a little. I gladly accept and am happy that I can help out this time.

I meet all of his guests, including their girlfriends, of which some are fascinating women. There

is the possibility that some of them could live here someday. Wouldn't that just be fantastic?

Carlton reveals a fun and enviable surprise to his guests at the dinner party; his Swan 60 sailboat is en route and should be in Jepara sometime in the next few weeks. "WOW! You have a Swan sailboat—a sixty-footer—and it's coming here?! Awesome!"

We learn that it has been en route for months now. Carlton has owned her for more than ten years and has many, many stories to share with us but wants to keep the party focused on us, his dinner guests. He'll share the stories another time.

I don't know much about sailboats, but I do know a lot about boats in general. I know a Swan is known for its leading technology and its aesthetic flair. It's a gorgeous, sleek, and expensive sailboat; I'm beside myself with excitement! This archipelago has more than seventeen thousand islands, maybe I will get to see more of them.

It was an entertaining and lively night as always at Carlton's house. It was even better enjoying the companionship of engaging and exotic Western women.

It's only a few weeks later when Carlton invites me and other expats along with their mates out on

his sailboat for a Sunday cruise. I've gone from the arduous jungle to splendor in only a few weeks. We spend the day cruising on the Java Sea, in these cool and bright clear turquoise waters, under vivid blue skies with gentle and soft breezes. Some people are terrified, some get deathly seasick, some get drunk; it's only Carlton and me standing at the end of the day. I'm in a place that seems the end of the world, and suddenly, there is a yacht available to me. I'm on cloud nine!

All of us are invited each Sunday for a cruise; the guests dwindle quickly as most never get their sea legs. Each time I'm out on the Swan, Atos is on the boat too. During this time, Atos helps me to learn other essentials to improve the quality and appeal of my furniture. Atos is hugely supportive of me, and I respect his business skills tremendously. But eventually, it's Carlton and I who possess the true love of the ocean. I was born in the sign of water, and it is there that I feel my best, away from everything so I can breathe. Carlton begins teaching me more about the ocean and sailing. My thirst to maneuver and explore the oceans and seas steadily grows. I feel like I'm one with the universe and in sheer bliss while on the high seas.

I start questioning Carlton about how he had come to own this yacht and the stories he promised to share. I learn that Carlton had this boat in the Caribbean and used it to smuggle drugs into America for more than ten years. He only left because he got the feeling that his luck was about to run out. He had sufficient money to go to Bali and live forever. He eventually made his way to Jepara, starting his furniture and antique business. The dude is truly an entrepreneur. Good grief, drug money! Gjeeshk, sorry I asked! My interest faded as quickly as it had blossomed. But my love for the high seas never waned.

Ramadan is here, and Idul Fitri (Eid al Fitr) is just around the corner. This is the time of year when more than a billion Muslims around the world begin a month of dawn-to-dusk fasting, which is the main component of Ramadan, the ninth month of the Islamic calendar. The fasting Muslims associate the holy month with complete abstinence from food, drink, smoking, and sexual relations during daylight hours. As the month of Ramadan draws to a close, everyone scans the sky for the appearance of the new moon marking the end of the month of fasting. News of the sighting is traditionally conveyed by an announcement from the mosque, along with televi-

sion and radio coverage. This is the signal for the start of Idul Fitri, meaning the Feast of Breaking the Fast. In Central Java, the law requires *all* businesses to close for ten days, with only a few exceptions. The masses head home to their villages. The expats do a mass exodus as well because their businesses have been forced to close, and they want to avoid the severe chaos and gridlocked roads. This same pandemonium is all over Southeast Asia. But to me, this equates to a forced two weeks of vacation each year! YEA!

I plan to return to Phuket, Thailand for Eid; however, I don't realize that this year, Eid coincides with the Chinese New Year, which is another mass exodus that generates chaos of its own. I can't get a reservation to anywhere. I finally get a stand-by flight to Singapore, stay a night and get another stand-by flight to Phuket. The Phuket and Trang provinces includes ninety-nine of the most idyllic islands I have ever seen, even rivaling the Caribbean, recognized as "The Pearl of the Andaman Sea." The first time I went to Phuket, I spent my time on Patong Beach and at Phra Nang Beach in Krabi, Thailand. This time, I'm not going to be landlocked. The long-tail boat is a ubiquitous sight on the beaches of Phuket

and Krabi. It's the distinctive water transportation for Thailand, also known as the "gondolas of the South." They come in many shapes and sizes with hulls as long as thirty feet. They are usually covered most their length by a canvas awning, but always with a propeller attached to the end of a long pole, powered by enormous engines. The boatman raises and lowers the long "tail," changing its angle so it steers the boat while also propelling it.

I hire a young family man named Nit. He and his long-tail boat are going to be my water taxi for the next ten days. I tell Nit the islands I want to explore, and he gives me his list of must-see places. "Koh" is the word for "island" in Thai. Our list of kohs is in place, so Nit and I and my backpack start off to Maya Bay at Koh Phi Phi first. This is maybe one of the most beautiful bays on the face of this earth. It is a bay surrounded by hundred-meter cliffs three-quarters of the way around. There are several small beaches inside the bay with silky-soft, white-powder sand, and colorful underwater corals that are home to reef fish whose colors span the spectrum. Lining the cliffs and beach are coconut palms that seem to sway with a calming rhythm. Every time I turn the last corner and enter into Maya Bay, my breath is

taken away as its magnificence fills my being. A hidden clear lagoon backdropped with gargantuan stone faces: It would convince anyone there *is* a God. The bad news is that it is so beautiful and so well-known, many boats are hired to ferry tourists to Maya Bay, creating a scenario of hundreds of moored boats tied side by side, and others still trying to enter into the bay. The trick is getting to the bay in the early morning to appreciate its beauty in peace before the multitudes of people arrive.

Nit and I zigzag across the Andaman Sea, hopping from one island to the other for ten days: Koh Yao Noi, Koh Racha, Koh Lanta, and Koh Jum. Every island is as awesome as the last. When I think I can't see a prettier bay or beach, it materializes before my eyes, just a different kind of exquisiteness. Each island has at least one little hut serving up the best Thai cuisine one could imagine. I order a feast, more than I can ever eat, all for five dollars. And for another three dollars, each hut also sells the pints of local Mekong whisky. Mekong whisky, ginger ale, and a squeeze of lime. Oooh la la!

I can't help but notice all the young people so laid-back and happy, so relaxed on the beaches and at the little food huts; then I realize that it isn't

cigars they are smoking but cigar-size reefers! Maybe I should have made time in college for these types of things.

I spend the last evening of my adventure with Nit and his family and friends. I'm giving it my best to enjoy our meal; it certainly isn't the marvelous Thai cuisine I've been enjoying. I inquire what it is that we are eating since I'm not familiar with the dish. "Dried hornets, you like?"

I know that I will be back to these islands again and again. And maybe someday, it will be in my own boat. Wouldn't that be the greatest thing ever?

My flights home have me spending the night in Singapore again. I inquire with the concierge where can I find a high-quality hair salon. I'm told that there's a new Toni & Guy salon that's been getting good reviews. I make an appointment and go.

At the salon, I tell the young man that I only want a trim, to clean up my hair after spending so much time in the sun and saltwater.

"Ma'am, I think you would look good with short hair, you should consider a short style," says the stylist.

"No. I don't want short hair."

"Well, short hair is really in right now."

distraction

"No, thank you, a trim only please, with some texturizing here and here. Do you know how to do texturizing?"

"A Princess Diana hairstyle is really popular; I think you would look great in that style."

"No, I don't want a hairstyle that looks like someone else. Enough of the short hair talk, please."

"Are you sure?"

"Yes, I'm sure," I say with certainty.

The stylist takes a large grasp of my long hair which falls halfway down my back, holds it up, and *CLIP!* He cuts about fifteen inches of my hair in one cut, creating a huge gap in the back of my head.

"What the hell did you do that for?!" I exclaim rather loudly.

"Well, now you have no choice but to go to a short style; I promise you will be happy," he says smiling and with confidence.

I am furious! I see red! But I don't see what other choice I have now but to continue. I warn, "If I don't like it, I'm not paying!"

"Okay."

Well, I freaking hate my Princess Di haircut! I grab some magazines to find a short style I could live with. By the time it is all over, my hair is so short, it

is above my ears. I did *not* pay when storming out of the salon. What a crummy end to an incredible vacation.

On returning home, it isn't long before my attentions are needed elsewhere, and I just avoid mirrors for years to come. I did learn that it is much easier to wash my boyish short hair in a cold mandi. Maybe it was meant to be.

13

Ron Let's Go
2008

By midmorning, Huda searches and finds me in the factory. He tells me that the tax department called to schedule our audit. "Gjeeshk, it hasn't even been forty-eight hours, that's not a good sign. Have you heard any other information from your contacts?" Satrece asks Huda.

"I've spoken to our consultant, *Bapak Pajak*, or Mr. Tax Man. You know that he is the head of the tax department," Huda replies.

I can't help but laugh out loud with his statement, only in a Third World country is your paid consultant also the boss of the department responsible for auditing you. "Yes, I know," I say smiling.

"Well, Bapak Pajak is very worried. The auditors have been brought in from the outside, and he doesn't know them, nor does he understand WHY *they* were brought in."

"Huda, since I haven't been involved with our local taxes, do we have anything to be worried about?" I inquire, already knowing the answer.

"If Bapak is worried, I'm worried," Huda exclaims.

"What could be the worst-case scenario?" I further inquire.

"I don't know Ms. Satrece…I just don't know," Huda says, looking away and shaking his head.

As I step back into the office, Susi asks to speak with me. Susi's paying the monthly bills and informs me that the electricity bill is three times higher than normal; electricity has now increased as well. As Susi is paying and reconciling our expenses for the month, she notices that our expenses have increased more than three hundred percent over previous months, and says this is just the beginning.

As I look at the dire situation head on, I know I cannot leave the country right now and ignore all of these problems. They are not going away. I don't appreciate the additional pressure Ron has placed

on me; he has become a total distraction. I'm fully immersed as it is. It was already a stretch for me to agree to meet him in Jakarta for dinner, much less for a week's vacation. I just CANNOT leave next week; the decision is final. I find Ron very endearing, but in the end, he returns to America, and I'm still here; life goes on, simple as that. I want to let him down gently, at first through an e-mail, as I can better explain the entire situation that way. I go to my desk, open my laptop and begin typing an e-mail to Ron. I explain about the ongoing negotiations for the factory and grounds, the impending tax audit, Furniture Choices moving the date forward for them to visit the factory, bringing me designs for a new collection. Then I detail to Ron all the other numerous problems facing me. I admit that there is no way possible I can leave the country or travel as far as Vietnam. I can't be that far away from my business, nor can I be that much out of touch. I would have a difficult time enjoying myself; and it wouldn't be fair to him, or me. I take a deep breath, reread the e-mail and hit the Send button. It's done. Some pressure removed; I can focus now on saving jobs and saving my business.

Satrece

Ron finishes his meetings for the day and strolls back into his hotel room; checking his e-mail messages is the first thing on the list. After he completes his e-mails, he'll call Vietnam to finish the last reservations for their trip.

Most of the plans are already finalized, but there are a few finishing touches remaining, as Ron pays such close attention to detail. Satrece is going to love this trip, and she'll see the adventurous side of him too. More importantly, he will finally get to spend time with her to see if she is really everything she seems to be. As Ron fantasizes about the upcoming trip, he sees the two of them in Hanoi touring Halong Bay on a private river charter with the beautiful turquoise waters and the giant green monoliths jutting out from the bay. He can picture Satrece in a bikini with a tanned sleek body and them drinking champagne, having a picnic in the bay. Ron fantasizes them snorkeling and him helping her back into the traditional riverboat—for more sun and more champagne. Yes, it's going to be an enchanting and romantic trip, maybe a trip that will change his life forever.

Glancing at his computer, Ron sees an e-mail from Satrece and opens it first. Ron reads it and then reads it again. Jumping to his feet and exhaling deeply,

distraction

he looks up and closes his eyes, running his hands through his hair. Ron feels exasperated and heartbroken. He doesn't recall the last time he felt disappointment like this; on top of the world one minute and plunged into anguish and sorrow the next. He finds himself pacing the room thinking about the situation thoroughly. His next step could be the difference in whether or not he sees Satrece again. Ron reaches deep inside to gather up the strength to make the right decision for both of them. He feels he owes her that much, concluding that all he can do is to let her go, for now.

"Hello."

"Hi, Satrece. I've read your e-mail; have you seen my response yet?" Ron asks somberly.

"No, I haven't. So…you've read mine though? What are your thoughts about it?"

Ron musters his courage, "Well, your only choice is to manage your business. You just can't do it; you can't go. With everything that you say is happening, there's no way you can leave. The timing *is* all WRONG. You haven't shared with me all of these challenges that you are facing. I just wish there were something I could do for you. You could never enjoy yourself at this time, and I won't be the guilty one

taking you away from your responsibilities. If it is really these issues and not *me*, then I will see you the next time I'm here. I am not giving up on you just yet."

Satrece can't believe what she has just heard. Ron is letting her go, and he understands the bigger picture. Based on past experiences with men, she fully expected him to tell her that none of these issues were important, and she should be focusing on the reunion with him. However, this man is genuinely concerned for her and has her best interests at heart. He is truly one of a kind.

Satrece reassures Ron, "It IS these issues and the timing...I promise."

Satrece then attempts to lighten the conversation, "Under different circumstances, I would go, but I would STILL have my reservations that you are basically a stranger," Satrece says with a small laugh.

Ron isn't laughing. "I have to be honest with you, I'm extremely disappointed, but it is you that I am worried about. Are you sure there is nothing I can do for you?"

"There isn't a thing you can do for me; it will all work itself out in time. I've had some pretty tough situations in my years here; it always works itself out,

and it will this time too. But, Ron, thank you. Thank you for understanding."

"I don't see that I really have a choice."

"Well, at least you have planned a fantastic trip. I'm sure you will enjoy Vietnam."

"Oh, I'm not going without you. It was never about the trip or the new country; it was always about you and me spending time together, about us getting to know each other better. I'll start changing my itinerary immediately to return home once my business is finished. Well, in the morning anyway, but I will start cancelling the reservations in 'Nam right away. Maybe I'll be very successful here and have another business reason to return soon."

Satrece thanks Ron again for being so understanding and hangs up the phone. She thinks, *I do feel IMMENSELY relieved. One less issue to deal with, one more wolf shot at the door, one less thing to worry about. And at least I know now that he isn't a stalker…nor unreasonable…and a true businessman. I'm anxious to end the day at the factory and escape home; I'll read Ron's e-mail when I have privacy.*

As soon as I enter my home, I boot up my laptop to read Ron's full response. His e-mail mostly reiterates what he said on the phone, but I can now see

the raw emotion he had been so cleverly concealed. He is crushed, but he found the inner strength to let me be free. My lightened state is suddenly burdened again. I remember a motto that I have always admired, something like "If you truly love someone, let them go free. If they come back, they're yours; if they don't, it was never meant to be."

This, however, seems that "it was never meant to be."

14

Whirlwind
1997–1998

*I*t becomes a happy time for me when I go to the bank and see the rupiah foreign exchange rate compared to the U.S. dollar drop and drop. This means I'm making more profits per container, and the money is going further and further. Then I realize VAST drops are happening. Still living in a time warp, hardly having access to sufficient news, I decide to make a point to learn what's transpiring.

I learn that the U.S. has recovered from the recession in the early nineties, and interest rates are on the rise to head off inflation. This makes the U.S. a more attractive investment destination relative to

Southeast Asia, which had been attracting hot money flows, but it was now raising the value of the U.S. dollar. There are a number of contributing factors creating a domino effect of critical confluence in Asian countries that leads to this 1997 Asian financial crisis. Some economists are claiming that the advancing growth of Chinese exports is contributing to the other ASEAN nations' slowdown. Another possible cause of the sudden risk shock is the handover of Hong Kong sovereignty in July.

This all results in debacles of economic bubbles, massive withdrawals of credit to these crisis-wracked Asian nations, and exceedingly high levels of "capital flight," creating havoc on the already fragile economies. These distressed countries begin to unpeg their currencies from the high-valued U.S. dollar, which sends their currencies plummeting to never-seen-before depths. The rupiah had been valued at Rp 2,400 to the dollar and then dropped to four thousand, and it continued downward to six thousand, pausing at Rp 6,800 to the dollar, yet still kept tumbling. Indonesia announced that all banks ARE CLOSED for three days in efforts to slow the monumental capital flight. "Ruh Roh!" as Scooby Doo would say!

The inability of accessing my money and savings for three days sealed the deal for me to get *my* money out of the country too! NOTE: Plan a trip to Singapore cepat, cepat! Quickly, quickly!

Conversely, my profits continue to grow at a rapid pace. I'm receiving continuous faxes from people I'd never heard of "giving" me orders. My existing customers are having my invoices and letterhead stolen from their desks to learn where they're getting their furniture. The normal fax reads: "I WANT FURNITURE! MORE, MORE, MORE." Wow, life *is good*!

Before long, I begin to see the negative consequences. My workers, the villages, the island, the country, and the entire region are beginning to panic. The currencies are collapsing, and the people are NOT surviving. I call a staff meeting to fully comprehend the effects of the collapsing governments and currencies on the local people. The news is devastating. I am urged to spend the day walking around in the villages to fully understand. Huda and I do just that the next day. I see masses of people starving, people begging and sick people in all of the villages surrounding the factory. I had never seen anything like this before; I had done this walk many a time.

Satreee

I act immediately, putting a task force together of staff members and supervisors to assist me and decide what most urgently needs to be done to begin handling this critical situation. We give an immense salary increase in the factory effective immediately. Within a week, we have large trucks delivering to and subsidizing all the surrounding villages with the basics: the rice, flour, kerosene and other supplies essential to survival. Each family on the village roster receives "x" kilos of rice, "x" kilos of sugar, flour, etc. We feed the villages for nine months.

I send Huda on a reconnaissance, evaluating the welfare of the community, only to learn of disturbing developments, including that the foster home and senior care facility have people sick and starving, now with no electricity. The vast information gathered from this mission results in steady, monthly donations to the community—donations that don't end with the crisis but continue, and will as long as I have this factory.

This Asian crisis brings new expats chasing opportunities. Factories start popping up all over town bringing healthy employment for the multitudes that need work. More English people come, the French and Italians arrive, and the Dutch flood

the area. The Koreans and Japanese enter. I'm told that there are more jobs in our little town than over most of the country combined, an exaggeration of course, but the point is made. The jungle isn't so much like the jungle anymore; my "little secret" isn't so secret either. The government starts working on the infrastructure to support the efforts yielding so much employment. More electricity comes to town, and road projects begin. Jepara is becoming like the Wild West, complete with cowboys and outlaws. I hear the drug ecstasy has hit town, and the rumors go ballistic. I'm told tales of many people, including Atos, spending their weekends in suites in Semarang orchestrating wild orgies lasting forty-eight hours complete with swinging, switching, additions and whatever else anyone can imagine in their wildest fantasies. Jepara now has sex, drugs and rock and roll!

Business continues to thrive so much that I pay off my credit card debt, all $40,000. I assist and aid the villages in any way or in anything that I can do. My prior seducing and bribing pay off, and I get more electricity, all that I will ever need.

I decide to focus my energies with Huda's help on renovating my home compound. I find and hire a local architect. We change the pitch of the roof and

add decorative roof tiles supported by traditional hand-carved Javanese teak columns and rafters. I get solid cement walls, instead of the layer of bricks I previously had, lay ceramic floor tiles and install a real shower and basin along with hot water in my bathroom! I add full-length French doors that will keep the green mambas out as well as French windows in my sleeping quarters. I'm actually able to find and add floor carpeting to my bedroom and then install air conditioners in my bedroom and office!

Rifan becomes my personal supervisor of the home construction project while I'm working at the factory. The construction is estimated to take three to four months to complete, so I move into a little two hundred-year-old caretaker's house on the factory grounds. My workers attempt to convince me not to move there because the house is haunted by a Japanese man from World War II. Each morning I enter the factory, I'm studied and watched, with workers ascertaining whether I've been possessed by the ghost who lives there.

I wake in the caretaker's house one morning as sick as I can be with a burning fever. My sheets are soaked, and I'm miserable, maybe the sickest I've ever been. I attempt to get up and shower, but col-

lapse, eventually crawling back to bed. I'm so sick, I lie there, moaning and groaning, rolling from side to side, burning up one moment and shivering the next. I have a busting headache, I ache in every joint; do I have the flu? If so, it's the worse flu that I've ever had. Ningseh and Rifan are at the house overseeing the renovations; I know the people from the factory are about five hundred feet away but are giving me my privacy. I need help; I need some water. Hours pass, I feel just as miserable. Finally in the afternoon, I hear someone banging on my front door. I yell but don't have the strength to yell loud enough. I try to get to the door; the knocking has stopped. I make it to the door and get it opened to see Sholikin walking off in the distance. "Sholikin, Sholikin," I mutter out. He hears something, turns and sees me. It seems Sholikin is the only one brave enough to venture to the haunted house to check on me. It's been the concern and gossip all day at the factory; where am I? What's happened to me? My illness proves that the ghost haunts the house! The ghost *got* me!

The closest doctor that I just MIGHT, maybe trust, is in Semarang. I can't see a trip to Semarang as being an option. I'm too sick to get there. My workers put a group together to care for me and check

on me. I understand there are only a few volunteers due to the presence of the ghost. They all love me and want to help, but the *ghost*?! I hardly remember the next several days. Sholikin comes every day to sit with me. Sholikin announces to me that I'm *yellow*, so now I have no choice; I must go to Semarang to the hospital.

The next morning, Huda loads me up and takes me to the Semarang hospital. I'm diagnosed with malaria. I'm too sick to understand anything the doctor says, so Huda stays at my side. They want to admit me into the hospital. *Are you kidding me?* I'm thinking to myself, this place reminds me of a large Ratu Shima Hotel. No way. I insist that Huda take me to the Ciputra Hotel, the nicest hotel in Semarang, which isn't that nice. For a fee, the doctor will visit me at the hotel regularly as needed. I stayed at the Ciputra Hotel for the next week recovering and getting my strength back. My advice, don't ever let yourself get malaria!

With the house renovations completed, life still isn't getting back to normal. The roads are getting more crowded and more lawless. I decide to send Rifan to driving school; a personal driver only makes

sense with the roads becoming insane. Rifan has proven himself smart, dependable, and trustworthy. After I finish work each evening, I go out with Rifan, so he can practice driving and I can teach him the Western way of driving. I think Rifan is the only driver in Indonesia that does shoulder checks, uses his rearview mirror, doesn't drive down the center of the road, and actually uses his blinkers.

Triggered by extreme rising prices, food short-ages and extensive unemployment, violent riots erupt across the nation. The economic problem is compounded by a political uncertainty because the election in 1997 is marred by widespread cases of voter rigging causing public outcry, especially among supporters calling for the government to follow a democratic process. Incidents of mass violence, including of a racial nature, occur throughout Indonesia. The main target of violence is the ethnic Chinese as their shops are looted and burned. Other attacks on foreigners are reported in this mad craze. It is reported that more than a thousand people have died in the riots, at least 168 cases of rape are reported, and material damages are valued at more than Rp 3.1 trillion (US$310 million). A group gathering of more than ten thousand people at the Trisakti University

incites a plan to march to the Parliament building. The marches are headed off but accounts emerge of students being shot. This is the catalyst of the whirlwind that changes the history of Indonesia forever.

This leads to the resignation of President Suharto, who had ruled the country as an authoritarian ruler since 1966. Even with his departure, political uncertainty remains. The newly appointed President Habibie, along with most of his cabinet, are known as cronies of Mr. Suharto, with no political base.

Indonesia finds itself gearing up for yet another election, this time a *Democratic* election. Having never had free elections in Indonesia, soon there are forty-eight parties organized and daily campaigns of motor scooter parades battle the other parties' motor scooter parades for space on the roads. Some parties are dressed in flannel pajamas printed with teddy bears and others' outfits have taken on the visual characteristics of pirates. Believe me, when you get stuck in a campaign of this sort, you would much rather be caught with people wearing teddy bears versus the ones wearing pirate outfits! And you definitely don't want to be caught in the group Rifan and I refer to as the "Greenie Meanies," the Muslim reli-

gious faction wearing all green that is the most malicious of all.

As the riots grow, for safety reasons, I allow Ningseh and Rifan to take the vehicle home each night. I won't let them be stranded on the roads waiting for buses that aren't coming. I notice now each morning when Rifan enters, his bright smile is withering. After a few days, I ask Ningseh if Rifan is feeling sick.

"No, he's not sick."

"Do you know what the problem is?"

"He's tired."

"Tired from what?"

"Sleeping in the mobil."

Mobil is Bahasa for car, and is pronounced more like *mo bill.*

"Sleeping in what mobil?"

"Your mobil."

"Why is Rifan sleeping in my mobil?'"

"To protect it."

"Protect it from what?"

"From all the crimes and chaos that are happening. It's now the only car in the village through these hard times, and Rifan can't let anything happen to it, so he's sleeping in it every night to protect it."

Good grief! I think I'm doing something thoughtful and kind for them, but I've only made their lives more complicated. Rifan insists, however, that he still wants to drive the "mobil" home each night.

Now on a daily basis, the SUV is getting pummeled and pounded by the rioters. The windshield and windows are getting beat upon by hands and sticks. Rifan is always the driver through these trying times, and it's his responsibility to protect me. He knows he'll have to answer to a lot of people if he lets something happen to "Ms. Satrece." He ingeniously buys two sets of paraphernalia representing all forty-eight parties. Whenever we get caught in a riot (many times each day now), we roll the windows down and hang the flags or banners or whatever we have for this political party and shout their slogans and wave *their* things. Rifan's plan works brilliantly—for a while.

Eventually, I am contacted by the ABRI or the Indonesian National Armed Forces (to which I make monthly donations for extra security) and am told to evacuate Java, that the riots are beyond their control, and word is "the worst" is yet to come. I decide to neglect their warnings because I have so many fur-

niture orders, and my factory is growing so rapidly. Soon, the chaos and disorder reach the point that one day, Rifan shouts for me to crawl into the back of the SUV and hide under a blanket. Well, maybe it's time for me to take that forced vacation after all. Sure, I'd love to go to Bali and hang out for a while; what's the matter with me?

I hire Sofie into my staff before I leave, making her my customer support liaison. Huda and Susi are going to need all the help they can get in my absence. Sofie speaks, reads and writes English fluently, which will help me tremendously as I manage the factory from another island.

Before it's over, a good portion of our town is looted and burned, with several deaths. I had to evacuate two more times before the madness ended.

15

A Change of Heart
2008

After reading the reply e-mail from Ron, I close my laptop and change my clothes to meet Ali. Ali is my fitness trainer; we have a standing appointment to work out together a minimum of three times a week and sometimes four, and on the other days, I treadmill alone in my gardens. Ali took courses in Semarang to become an American certified personal trainer and now has made personal training his full-time business. I have contributed to his knowledge by paying for his other certification courses offered on DVD. I turned half of my air-conditioned office into a fitness room. Now, most of my equipment is purchased and suffi-

cient enough, but I remember the times when most of it was handmade by Ali and me. We have grown to be good friends through the years. Ali speaks English quite well and trains several other expats who have recently relocated to Jepara to open furniture factories. More often than not, the expat men just want a buddy to hang out with while drinking beer and frequently cancel their workouts, having Ali to chitchat with, but still pay Ali his fee. Ali is likable, and I take my workouts seriously; we have created a gratifying repartee.

Ali enters the fitness room, and we begin stretching, and as always, he updates me on recent events around town and the local gossip. Ali quickly perceives my "distance" and lack of interest in the small talk this evening. He asks if I'm okay and wants to know what's wrong. He tells me that he doesn't like seeing me without my shine, how my light has turned to darkness.

What shine, what darkness, and what the heck is Ali talking about? Why the fables? I'm not exactly one to share my feelings, nor do I want to dump all the irritations and dilemmas of the business on him that he already knows. I continue to exercise, but quietly with higher intensity than normal. *What HAS*

Satrece

happened to my so-called light? I ask myself. An hour passes, but I don't notice. I say very little throughout our workout. I find myself needing his emotional support while still respecting my silence, but I seem to be going for bust with this workout. I finally notice how I'm drenched in sweat, and that Ali is rivaling to keep up with me today. We have worked out for two hours, and suddenly I realize my entire body is trembling. As we part ways and I hobble to the shower, I acknowledge to myself that I have exhausted my body with this Herculean workout. Afterward, I find myself pushing my food around on my plate throughout dinner. At last I discern an elusive deep sense that I have made a horrible mistake. My brain is numb, revealing nothingness, but my essence is searching for the offense.

Feeling, without thinking, I reach for the telephone to call Ron, "Hi. What are you doing?"

"I'm planning my departure. I've successfully cancelled all of our reservations and am now determining my new schedule in lieu of meetings that have been added."

"I see." Then a long silence fills the line. "I've been thinking …"

212

"What have you been thinking?" Ron says, sounding somber.

"I've been thinking that since you planned your trip here and managed to come all this distance, it would be a shame if I didn't make it to Jakarta for a date with you. How do you feel about that?"

"Are you sure? Are you *certain* this is the right thing for you to do?" Ron's excitement grows.

"If you still want me to…and you let me do it on my terms…it *is* the right thing to do," Satrece assures Ron. "I will be one manageable plane trip away if something else spirals out of control, and I'm needed back urgently."

"When would you like to plan this for?"

"Well, I've been trying to get a hold of Roger from Furniture Choices to ascertain his dates, but it seems he has fallen off the face of the earth. Can I let you know tomorrow after I see further how things are going? Also, you said that you've added some meetings; when will you now be available?"

"Okay, we have a little time to figure this out. My schedule now frees up next Wednesday."

"Well…I will *try* to take a couple days during the week and a weekend, but as you know, it's out of my control."

"I will happily take whatever time you can give me or whatever you can make happen." Ron is reserved but elated once again.

After Ron and Satrece talk a little more, they finish their conversation, and Satrece sits alone in front of her fountains reflecting, meditating on Shiva and discussing with her trio of kitties what has just happened.

I hadn't made a conscious decision to call Ron or to ask *him* on a date. But I think that's what I just did. I simply followed my heart, and that's where it led me. I hadn't seen that one coming! Once this man entered my world, things certainly got more complicated. *He is a distraction!* But maybe, just maybe, *he's a good distraction*.

I try several more times to reach Roger.

Huda and I meet the next morning. We decide on our next strategy to present for the nego renewing the lease on our building and land. We both conclude the audit is in Huda's hands for now. I figure out ways to advance our next round of uncertainties. I have successfully freed myself up and assigned David, my brother, to be my eyes and ears at the factory. David is elated.

The next day when Ron and I speak, I agree to meet him on Wednesday. I will travel to Semarang and fly onward to Jakarta that day. We agree to meet for cocktail hour and then dine together that evening; the places are to be determined. Ron then asks me what airline I would normally use to travel to Jakarta and what hotel I would normally book. *What an odd question,* I think. I tell him that I only fly Garuda Airlines domestically, and if it's business, I would stay at the Le Meridien Hotel, and if it's pleasure or a get-out-of-jungle break, I would stay at the Ritz-Carlton to pamper myself.

The following day, Ron telephones once again filled with excitement. "I've taken the liberty of booking your airline ticket and a room for you at the Ritz-Carlton Pacific Place. I hope that's okay."

"You've done what? I've lived here for fifteen years, and I am very capable of making my own airline and hotel reservations! Why did you do that?" Satrece asks, feeling offended. I'm not going to be indebted to him nor anyone else. Good grief, this man is a handful. "And you mean the Ritz-Carlton Kuningan," Satrece adds.

"I just wanted to do something nice for you; it seems you take care of the rest of the world…I

thought it would be nice if someone did something for you for a change. And no, it's not the Ritz Kuningan, it's the Ritz-Carlton Pacific Place, it's newly opened and extremely nice."

"Well, thank you, but no thank you. It's unnecessary. I will make my own reservations. There's a new Ritz-Carlton in Jakarta? And you know about this and I don't, how is this possible? Are you *sure* it's not Kuningan?" Satrece asks in disbelief.

Ron is amused, and Satrece is pouting when they hang up. Ron asks Satrece to at least think about his offer. Ron sees she is an obstinate one but truly admires her independence.

Satrece storms out of her bedroom and stomps to where David is enjoying his cigar. "What's the matter with you?" David asks.

"You won't believe what this guy just did. He has made both my plane and hotel reservations for me. Can you believe it?"

"So what? What's wrong with that? I bet he's just tryin' to do something nice for you."

"That's exactly what he said. But I don't like it!"

"Damn, sis, you're always doing things for everybody else; why don't you just let someone do somethin' nice for you for a change?"

"That's what he said too. Whose side are you on?"

David chuckles. "Yours, of course. So allow him to get your hotel room, and you get your plane ticket in case you need to hightail it out of there… either way, away from the dude or because you're needed back here."

"You really think I should allow him to get my room? You think that's wise?"

"What are you afraid of, sis? Go. Enjoy yourself and allow the dude to do something for you."

Once Ron returns to Jakarta from Singapore, he calls Satrece as soon as he is in the Silver Bird taxi.

"My brother says I should let you handle my room reservations, but I will make my own airline arrangements."

Ron, upbeat, says, "Well, I like your brother already, he's a wise man."

"By the way, my passport should be at your hotel when you get there."

"Yes, I'm aware. I will get it into my possession as soon as I get to the hotel. I'll let you know immediately as soon as it is safely in my hands."

"At least now you don't have to open the packet since we aren't going to Vietnam," Satrece says somewhat commandingly and relieved. My passport in Ron's hands is too much knowledge too quickly for my comfort level.

Ron laughs. "Yes, you're correct about that; I've already thought about it too."

Several hours later, Ron telephones again. "The Shangri-La has sent the courier packet containing your passport back against my instructions and after further confirming with the hotel while I was in Singapore. Your passport is…in…transit to…somewhere. I'm really sorry. I have everyone working on it and am promised that I will have it in my hands soon. I've done all that I can to move the world on this issue; it will be okay."

Satrece's deafening silence on the other end of the phone makes the point loud and clear for Ron. This is not a laughing matter; he understands the gravity of the issue, so she chooses not to add to his torment.

Ron sighs, "I thought it would already be back in my hands by now…Where are the competent people in the world today? Don't worry, I will get it. I won't stop until it's in my possession."

"I'm going to hold you to that," Satrece adds as she hangs up the phone.

Ron has the passport courier packet in his hands within the next forty-five minutes, and he phones Satrece to apprise her that all is in control and no worries.

Back in his room at the Shangri-La Hotel, Ron is at his computer working on correspondence, while all the time the courier packet is distracting him. Gravitating to the package, Ron picks it up to examine it. He can't help but gauge the bulkiness and questions why it's so thick? He continues to scrutinize the packet, his thoughts focused solely on Satrece. Ron is inquisitive to look at the passport photo and curious of her age. Hmmm…he studies it and begins to formulate ideas as to how old she is. Listening to her stories and timeline, Ron has an age in mind, but she looks much younger, maybe mid-thirties. Doing the math and considering her accomplishments, she must be older than that, but she certainly doesn't look it. Holding the envelope like a precious gem, Ron tries to determine Satrece's birth date. Pondering it, suddenly the dates come, first the month of January, then a specific date, January 20 appears vividly in his

mind. He further ponders the year in which she was born, and clearly, the vision materializes. It's like he's just gazed into a crystal ball, and he knows precisely how old she is, Ron attempts to convince himself. This packet holds the answers to many of his questions, but if he opens it, how would he explain that to Satrece?

"You are too cute!" Ron gushes into the phone.

"What are you talking about?" Satrece asks.

"The Post-it with the smiley face you stuck over your passport picture, how cute is that!" Ron laughs.

"You opened my passport, how dare you?" Satrece replies, shocked.

"I know…I'm sorry, but I just couldn't help it. It kept calling my name, and then it spoke to me," Ron says frivolously.

"What did it have to say to you?" Satrece is now smiling, hearing Ron's infectious laughter.

"It told me your exact birth date, and I guessed the date you were born down to the day and year!"

"That's just great!" Satrece says as ironically as she can imply, "That's precisely the data I wanted you to have right up front. And not to mention, I didn't want for you to see that lovely photo taken in Surabaya either," Satrece further chides.

220

Ron says, "It *is* a lovely photo, isn't it? Any particular reason for the smiley face hiding it? You are as lovely as I remember, but you still have me laughing."

"Yes, to hide that hideous picture. Surabaya technology at its finest. I look like I have blonde hair with a super fat face...it's only a *little* distorted."

"I can't help but to admire your passport, it's very thick. It's impressive and tells an amazing story. Wow, are you ever well-travelled!"

"Now you have to settle the score."

"What do you mean?"

"When is your birthday, and where were you born?"

"Ah okay. It's only fair. But you need to know, you look much younger than your age. I only guessed it based on stories you have told me."

"Dude, I'm still not letting you off the hook... offer up."

16

The Ocean, Sea, and Me
1999

With all debts paid, savings account replenished, a nice cushion in the business bank account, house remodeled, and the factory rockin' and rollin', it's time to pursue my next calling. I contact every boat broker I can find in Jakarta, Singapore, and Thailand, consulting them on what kind of boat would meet my needs for cruising the Indonesian archipelago and, possibly later, Southeast Asia; and by the way, do you have one for sale? It's pointed out to me that I'll have no Coast Guard to come to my rescue, and I will never know where I'll be able to find fuel next; there will be no weather marine reports available, no

marked channels and no published cruising guides, only mostly uncharted waters with the exception of the local fishermen. Sounds like my type of adventure, where do I sign up?

I buy *Lady Satrece* a 45-foot DeFever Motor Yacht with twin inboard engines, three sleeping cabins, a galley, and a head. I learn that this type of pleasure cruising yacht represents the best legendary quality and renowned dependability: it's well built, reliable, economical, and cozy. She's been sitting in the Royal Singapore Yacht Club for the last decade only being used for Yacht Club karaoke parties and charitable benefits. Her engines are good, but she needs a lot of aesthetic work, her electronics need to be updated, and her hull needs treating. She has a beautiful and graceful large flared bow, teak railing, floors, and swim platform. She's white with a navy accent trim up top and a deep red waterline. She's graced with character and style.

I decide to hire Mick and Yavette Wagner, an English couple from East Africa, newly retired from Her Majesty's Royal Navy. I haven't had a vacation other than Ramadan for a few years now with the business growing so steadily. I decide that I need Westerner help in the factory and know I need imme-

diate expertise to get *Lady Satrece* in tip-top shape. They both are hired as a team with the strategy that Yavette will start in the factory immediately as my understudy, learning from me, and Mick will oversee the renovations of the boat in Singapore. He also has the knowledge to teach me everything I need to know about yachting; then he will eventually come to work in the factory.

Once the renovations are underway, Mick begins outfitting *Lady Satrece* with dinghy and motor, automated and paper charts, safety equipment, new sleeping mattresses, and new awnings, additional anchors and chain, radios, and binoculars, handheld GPS units, and round one of deep-sea fishing equipment, etc. It makes my head spin knowing how much I need to learn.

It's finally time to bring *Lady Satrece* home to Java in June 2000. Mick will be the captain, I will be the first mate, and we hire two other experienced hands, John and Abu Bakar. Our trip from Singapore to Java will entail going through the Singapore Strait, into Batam, Indonesia to clear Immigration and Customs. We will then journey through the Riau Strait into the South China Sea, southward to the Bangka Strait (or pirate straits off the coast of Sumatra), and into the

Java Sea, then on toward Jepara. The renovations for *Lady Satrece* took longer than estimated for various unavoidable reasons; now this journey home will be perilous because the winter easterly trade winds associated with high pressure, and the equatorial trough, will be in full swing. There is normally an equatorial trough associated with showers and squalls in this area but add the stronger winter trade winds from June through August, and this means the swells can be six to ten feet with a Beaufort Wind Force of four to six, meaning winds of about fourteen to twenty-four knots. Looks like we are going to give *Lady Satrece* a true test ride on her maiden voyage, and I'm about to get an advanced degree in "Captaining a Yacht."

This is just the beginning of my adventures to come, and it is my *dream come true*, or one of them anyway! My crew and I are quickly becoming known in Singapore, as people learn of us completing the final preparations of *Lady Satrece* and purveying for this journey home to Java. In preparing for our seafaring travels, we learn how unchartered these waters are and how few yachts have actually made this journey.

We break the customary bottle of champagne over her bow the night before we leave. Tomorrow

is only to Batam; this leg of the journey will only take about four to five hours. We will be going into Nongsa Point Marina to clear Indonesian Customs and Immigration, where we will be in the hands of the CIQ (Customs, Immigration & Quarantine) police. We are forewarned that this could take up to twenty-four to forty-eight hours.

We depart Singapore about 10:00 a.m. as port clearance and immigration with the harbormaster was longer and slower than anticipated. While Mick worked on the clearance for all of the crew onboard *Lady Satrece*, I found a Singaporean Regional Meteorological Weather website. The weather looks pretty good for the next two to three days for this time of year. The four-hour cruise to Batam is uneventful; everyone learns their positions, and Mick is in awe of *Lady Satrece* and the electronics we chose. With the most sophisticated GPS radar chartplotter available integrated into the autopilot system, navigating *Lady Satrece* is a piece of cake. However, Mick insists on teaching me how to plot the paper charts, along with all rules, regulations, and safety procedures of Her Majesty's Royal Navy. He is intent that these rules and safety procedures are always followed under any and all circumstances. He will not be responsible for

me dying on the high seas. I agree and vow to Mick that my crewmembers and I will always be compliant to these rules while aboard *Lady Satrece*. I'm not ready to die either.

We change and hang our Indonesian flag as we leave the Singaporean waters and enter the Indonesian waters, as defined by international marine law. We follow all procedures and call the Marina VHF radio channel 72 for guiding assistance into the marina and temporary berthing. We know that the crew and passengers are not allowed to leave the vessel without CIQ clearance and approval. That doesn't mean that we can't swim in the turquoise blue waters or launch the dinghy into the water to learn and practice with it. It takes twenty-four hours for approval, so we plan our departure for early the next morning; if all goes as planned, we will not be on land again for at least four to five days. We have added four extra fifty-five-gallon fuel drums since we are neither yet knowledgeable nor experienced with our fuel consumption. We are as ready and prepared as we can be. The plan calls for two of us on deck and on watch at all times with two of us resting, when needed.

Satrece

In the mouth of the South China Sea, we officially pass over the equator about 11:00 that night. This is the accolade in which a sailor officially earns an earring, but I already have four earrings, so I'm set. The next day, further into the South China Sea, we catch our first fish with the baits or lures that we are pulling. Actually, to boast, I'm captain at the time, so Bakar actually catches the fish. It's sizable—a Queenfish—but not very edible I'm told. In the excitement of catching the fish, I speed the boat up instead of slowing it down, and I basically break the fish's neck. Though he is returned to the water, because of me, he is never to breathe again or gill again or whatever it is that fish do. Today, we see the most marine life of the trip. We see bountiful birds circling and diving into the water; they're diving for fish, so I learn this is a sign that the fish are here! We see a dolphin and a pit of yellow and gray stripped sea snakes. Then we see the most amazing thing: three WHITE dolphins trimmed in soft pink.

With the four of us onboard *Lady Satrece*, there are many years of sea experience, but none of us had ever before seen the elusive white albino dolphins! They are kind enough to escort *Lady Satrece* and swim alongside as we trawl, giving us an up close

look and a memorable experience. This has to be a good omen!

The weather and conditions don't allow us to drop another hook into the water for the duration of the journey. The swells are growing, the winds are blowing, and the clouds are gathering; and now we are entering the Banka Strait, known as the fourth most dangerous pirate waters in the world. We arrive at the mouth of the straits at dusk and decide to anchor for the night. We are heeding our directives, as we were warned and warned and warned to "Never, never, never! maneuver these straits at night because this is when the pirates are the most dangerous." We've calculated that it will take us twenty-four hours to navigate the straits, so Mick sends the two crewmembers to shore in the dinghy to find out the best place to anchor at the halfway point of the strait and to seek information about the weather. We anchor off of Muntok, Bangka, Sumatra, Indonesia; now that's a mouthful. The crew returns without success in gathering any information on either of the needed topics.

We begin day four sailing into the straits, an uneventful day other than the storms that are brewing. In the evening, Mick chooses a place about midway through the strait to anchor for the night. When

we attempt to anchor, we are on rocky ground, and the anchor will not catch, and he and Bakar try for more than two hours. After lots of discussion and failed attempts, we decide to proceed onward. So much for the warnings, the "NEVERS," the nights and the pirates. I don't know if Mick is rusty in the process of anchoring, or the rocky ground is truly the problem; however, my confidence in him is diminished. We decide that all four of us will be on watch for the night as we maneuver these dreaded straits. It's one hell of an eerie and memorable night. We watch storms and squalls in the distance seemingly everywhere, an imposing light show of thunder and lightning and gobs of rain as far as the eye can see.

As morning approaches, we are nearing the end of the straits. There is a U.S. shipwreck from World War II known to be in the area and supposedly marked, but as usual in Indonesia, it is not. It's 4:30 in the morning, meaning another hour until sunrise. We kill time for about an hour, so we can maneuver past the shipwreck in the daylight. It's the narrowest part of the channel, so no room for error. Still drawn to the rhythm of the sea, in the stillness of the dawn, yet another day is born. As 7:00 a.m. approaches, we are through the channel and filled with exhilaration.

We decide to anchor, and we are off the coast of Tobo Ali, Bangka. We haven't slept for twenty-four hours, and we need weather information before we can proceed, as the conditions are deteriorating. Just as we anchor, the storm we've been watching from afar hits with a fury. We'll just stay anchored and ride out the storm; I enter my cabin for a nap and to read for a bit.

With a break in the weather, I go ashore in the dinghy with the two crewmembers in search of weather information. When we land, having a new dinghy and a "shiny" new motor, I arrange for some locals to stand guard on the equipment. "Please don't let anything happen to it nor anyone touch it. Mengertti?" (Understand?) "Ya, ya, ya," we are assured.

I quickly perceive there haven't been too many five-feet ten-inch white women running around this island speaking Bahasa asking questions about the weather. All eyes are upon us!

"Need weather information?" they ask; everyone looks up in the sky and assures us it will rain big soon.

"No shit!" We learn that there are no television stations or Internet here on this island, so we realize

we aren't going to succeed in getting the information we need. I seek to find a cell phone signal, fifteen inquiries and four miles later, we find one. I call Susi at the office and begin the arduous task of talking her through the website I found in Singapore for the Meteorological Weather report. The Internet in the year 2000 is in remote Indonesia—in our factory—but it is still dial-up. As Susi and I work through this formidable task of searching for weather patterns on an unfamiliar website using archaic dial-up Internet, and me on a cell phone with little signal, another storm comes, and yet another storm goes. We begin our walk back to the dinghy as dusk approaches, and by now, a crowd of people line the roads to catch a look at us as though we are the parade. All the locals are waving at us and yelling out questions. "Dari mana?" (Where are you from?) "Pergi ke mana?" (Where are you going?) As I answer in Bahasa, the crowd smiles and claps while giving us a "thumbs-up." I'm thinking most people would have been horrified, but I have another fun experience to add to my repertoire.

With the pertinent need for weather information finally fulfilled, it is nightfall before we return to the dinghy. The weather is challenging; winds about

twenty knots, waves about six feet crashing on the shoreline, and the clouds hide any moonlight that might have helped us. I am very worried about the dinghy; will the people we hired still be standing guard? Will my boat in fact be there? Whew, it is. We are promised that no one has touched it, so the fishermen receive a very good payday.

As the three of us are pulling the dinghy into the ocean with massive strong waves crashing on shore, winds blowing and the night as black as it can be, we finally clear the last waves and are up to our chests in the seas. We hop into the dinghy; we made it! Dang it! Why won't this new motor start? The guys can't make sense of it, no reason for this. With the engine stalled and waves crashing, we nearly capsize. My backpack is thrown overboard, meaning some money, my cell phone, handheld radio, camera, lights, etc., are all in the ocean saltwater. Everything we have is lost or ruined. In an ungainly landing, we find ourselves back on shore.

Why did the engine stall? We figure out that the engine had been "admired" just a *little* too much today, drawing people from all around to see the "shiny" new motor. Every switch, setting, or choke that could have been tinkered with…had been! With

no light of any kind—no shore light, no moon-light, and now no flashlight—the local fishermen are holding their cigarette lighters for us to examine the engine. They're still so fascinated by the slick new engine they can't resist reaching over to pet the engine even now. Are we going to be stuck sleeping on the beach for the night in the storms? We are told there is a hotel close by; it's four dollars a night. I already know about a four-dollar room, and that you don't get much. That's the reason for *Lady Satrece*: to explore without having to stay in a four-dollar room. *Note to self: get that satellite phone I'd declined and find the waterproof packs.* When the guys are about to give up, they finally get the motor to work again. We had earlier radioed Mick that we were en route back to *Lady Satrece*, but there's no radio to inform him otherwise, and now it's a long time later. My handheld radio was drenched and as dead as it can be.

With the engine working properly, it's time to face the crashing waves again. This time, we have lightning assisting our vision, so we can see and time the waves better. This time, we have a successful departure, but without our spotlights, we have no lights to lead us back to *Lady Satrece*. So much for Royal Navy compliancy.

distraction

Once safely aboard *Lady Satrece*, I inform Mick of the weather bulletin. The waves in the Java Sea will be twelve to twenty feet high with scattered storms and squalls. Mick looks distraught and pops the top on yet *another* Bintang Beer. He explains to me that as soon as we get out of this strait and have no protection from the island of Bangka, we will be in extremely treacherous waters. From there, we are in the Java Sea at the entrance of the Sunda Strait. In these winter tradewinds, it's the absolute worst time of year to do this crossing; it will be fierce and formidable. I understand the Sunda Strait is the strait between the islands of Java and Sumatra, connecting the Java Sea to the Indian Ocean. I can only imagine the hazards that this alone can bring. Mick highly encourages us to forgo trying to reach Jepara in Central Java but to go to an alternate marina he knows of on the west coast of Java. Matter of fact, Mick's son is a professional captain of a large yacht there. His son could oversee *Lady Satrece* until we can get her home and maybe can help us find a full-time captain. I see the worried look on Mick's face, and I note the Bintangs he's throwing back. Yes, I agree, I have no interest in those large waves; a closer and safer location is the smart thing to do.

We will do this last leg straight through to Carita, about thirty hours to go. I'm beginning to feel the pangs of disappointment knowing that this voyage will soon be ending, but suddenly realizing this is *just the beginning* of many more adventures to come. I haven't worried about the factory; Yavette is there, able to handle any of the customer correspondence in English and to make wise Western decisions. *"Don't worry, be happy."*

We hit the West Java coast about twenty-four hours later with only three to four hours to go, southward bound. We get cell phone coverage, Mick calls his wife, and I call my brother in the States. We are safe and nearly at our destination. Beginning our sixth day at sea, we are three hours from berthing and the lights of Jakarta form the skyline ahead. Now in the Sunda Strait, we enter a very busy channel and extremely deep waters. Without warning and out of nowhere, we're hit by a massive storm and mammoth waves, a squall. We spend the last two hours of the trip hanging on for dear life. The boat—the star!— *Lady Satrece* handles the big storm and waves beautifully; never once did she alarm me, never once did I worry. Now I understand; she's a trawler, specially

designed for risky conditions and faraway journeys. She doesn't go *fast* but slow and steady and sturdy!

When we began our journey, Carita, West Java, wasn't an option; suddenly, it's our only option. By this point, my captain is celebrating and thoroughly drunk! *Oh shit*, I think, we still have to traverse the marina. Yet again, so much for Royal Navy compliancy.

Mick's son is awaiting our arrival at the marina and guides us in on the radio. All is well and good!

I spend the next several days in Carita hiring hands to maintain *Lady Satrece* and plan her homeward bound trip as soon as the weather allows. Jepara, here I come with my new toy!

17

"The Date"

*I*t is June of 2008. My flight on Garuda Airlines, GA237, from Semarang to Jakarta lands at Soekarno-Hatta International Airport on schedule at 12:45 p.m. I'm the first one off the plane; I grab a porter as I near baggage claim just as I have done a thousand times before. This time, however, I notice a uniformed fellow focused intently on me and swiftly advancing in my direction; he holds up a sign that reads "Madam Satrece." I flinch having recognized my name; then he swiftly seizes my computer bag from my porter and shoos him away, announcing that he is my escort and chauffeur. Oh, good grief, what have I gotten myself into now? As usual, Garuda Airlines treats me well, and my luggage is the first off. Then my hired driver snatches

my luggage, and with the upmost decorum quickly escorts me through the masses of humanity always swarming the Jakarta Airport. The crowd begins parting like the Red Sea with the chauffeur's serious bark and demeanor. All the eyes of the airport are on me, trying to determine who I might be. My luggage and I are loaded into a black Mercedes coupe; with hazard lights blinking the car hastily pulls away from the curb and enters the exit ramp out of the airport. The car and driver are proceeding with purpose and urgency; I look around trying to grasp what the purpose and urgency might be.

The driver immediately hands me his phone. "So I understand you have arrived safely in Jakarta and right on schedule," says Ron, the voice on the other end of the phone. "May I be the first to welcome *you* here this time?"

"Hi. Yes. Thank you. I can't believe you did this."

"I know…you are perfectly capable of arranging your own car and driver," Ron cleverly says.

"Of course I am, this was unnecessary," Satrece insists.

"Yes, but I wanted to. The driver says that you had no problems making contact?"

"No, he identified me long before I saw him."

"Of course, I told him you would be the most beautiful, tall American woman in the airport. He recognized you immediately," Ron says. I can hear the smugness in his voice, and I contemplate being annoyed or enticed, but either way, I'm not biting.

Ron continues, "Well, I've just finished the last of my work, so it's perfect timing. It's a shame that you're already here in Jakarta, and we don't have plans until later this evening…should we figure out something for us to do now?"

"No. Let's stick to the plan. My day started 'at prayers' this morning; it's already been a long day. I want to freshen up, and I haven't finished some urgent work that needs to be done."

"I understand. May I arrange for a manicure or a pedicure for you…or a hair salon appointment this afternoon?" Ron finds this all amusing.

I am not so amused. "Noo…If I want a manicure or pedicure or something, I will arrange it myself. I have work to do on my computer."

"Well, I can't wait to see you this evening. This day has finally come, I can't believe it," Ron says with the uttermost excitement.

I swear there's giddiness in his voice. "Me too," I reply, but I'm not feeling very sure about it all. "So exactly where is this new Ritz Pacific Place located?"

Ron says, "You are about to find out."

The driver and I enter the gates of a brand-new grand hotel, glistening in its full glory in the afternoon sun. It has luxury permeating from its every shiny beam with newness and freshness monopolizing the afternoon air. Goodness sakes, how did I not know this was here? The *boy* did *good*, I thought. As we pull up to the entrance, I notice there is a long welcome line of staff all practically standing at attention. I gauge the premises, wondering what diplomat or important VIP is visiting, with no flags or anything of interest in sight. The driver delivers me in front of the welcome line; I ask the driver to move up out of the way. He ignores me as he exits the car, and with my door open, he bows to me. As I turn stepping one leg out of the car door, I hear, "Ms. Satrece. Welcome." The words are echoed all the way down the welcome line as the line bows to me in a timed wave that is precisely executed. As my eyes focus on the staff while I'm exiting the Mercedes, the awareness seeps inward, I'm the VIP! They are here, greeting *me*.

Without having time to think but fully knowing who I'm going to clobber later this evening, I step to the head of the line and angle myself toward the entire group. I slowly and gracefully give my most cordial Asian bow, as I rise with a cordial smile matching their precision. "Terima Kasih," I say, thanking them.

The young lady at the head of the line holds her hand out while saying, "Ms. Satrece, I'm Yuti. I'm the head of guest recognition here at the Ritz-Carlton Pacific Place, and this is my assistant, Ms. Safi. We are here to make sure you have a wonderful and enjoyable stay with us. Please let us know of *anything* we can assist you with, or how we can make your stay better."

Neither young lady has smiled yet, but otherwise, their professionalism is top-notch. I say something charming to the girls, but still not the slightest smile. Each person in the line steps up to greet me; my concierge, my butler, my security manager, my personal housekeeping staff, my room service contact, my, my, my…woo…I'm dizzy. Each person meticulously looks me in the eyes, shakes my hand while saying my name and telling me what it is that they will do for me. Yuti and Safi each grasp one of my arms, and they whisk me away. They escort me

past security, past the registration desk, and we are heading for the large bank of elevators. I stop for a moment to admire the lobby and notice that the two ladies look as though they have the fear of God in them. I ask about registration only to be told it has been taken care of. My passport is already on file, and the appropriate signatures have been acquired. Oh yes, *my passport already on file.* I remember the clobbering I already have planned for Ron later.

We enter the elevators, and I try more banter in Bahasa, but the only response is uneasy stares. I try bantering in English, still nothing. Are these ladies judging me? Do they think I look as though I just came from the jungle, and are they reluctant to have me in their new glamorous hotel? What is going on? I'm whisked from the elevators onto the concierge level and explained my countless, numerous privileges. We enter another bank of elevators that will deliver us all to my room. As we near the door of the room, the girls stop at once. It is with Vanna White moves that they tell me this is the door to my room. What are you to say to that, nice door? I look at them quizzically. Yuti moves to the door, unlocks it, opens it slowly and peeks in.

Yuti then opens the door fully and enters, pulling me in as Safi is gently pushing. I take two steps into the room and stop dead in my tracks. To my surprise, I have entered my elegant corner room suite. Immediately, various effects are competing for my attention. With my consciousness not knowing where to begin, my eyes sweep to the right side of the room to begin a systematic survey. First, I see red roses, lots of them . . . several dozen. Beside the roses stands a gift bag elaborately decorated with bountiful tightly curled ribbons. In front of these two items stands a card addressed to "Darling Satrece." My eyes proceed over the various lovely amenities from the hotel and now focus straight ahead; I see a sofa with a coffee table in front of it. On the coffee table sits a newly made Cosmopolitan cocktail, chocolate-covered strawberries, fingertip sandwiches, and a bowl of exotic fruit. This light lunch has been attentively displayed, accompanied with a beautiful place setting for serving.

As my eyes sweep to the left side of the room, I see a counter-height horizontal shelf the length of the wall. It has blossomed into a generous and lavish bar setting. There are two silver buckets, one chilling a bottle of champagne, the other, several white

wines. A bottle of my preferred vodka, Grey Goose, sits among Grand Marnier, cranberry juice, along with other accoutrements that will yield the perfect Cosmopolitan cocktail. I see Russian standard vodka, green olives, crystal martini glasses, silver skewers, and a silver cocktail shaker, recognizing the makings of a dirty martini, and the garnishes for an exquisite presentation. With all my senses stimulated, alas I notice the soft romantic music playing in the room. I still haven't moved from my first two steps into the room, while all the time, I am keenly being observed by the ladies.

Yuti says, "What do you think, Ms. Satrece? Are you pleased? Do you like it?"

"Do I like it? I think Mr. Ron has outdone himself! I can't believe it…I'm…I'm absolutely speechless!" I look each girl in the face, and they see how awestruck I am. Seeing the pleasure on my face, unexpectedly, the ladies burst into giggles and start clapping their hands in jubilation. I now understand that the fear of God *had* been put into them…unless I was profoundly impressed, they hadn't done their jobs properly, and Mr. Ron would be very upset. They passed, I'm pleased, and Mr. Ron will be delighted!

Yuti says, "Mr. Ron must really adore you."

As it sinks in to me, "Yes, he must."

Yuti asks if she can tour me through the room, as she leads, and Safi escorts me to the right.

We enter a separate powder and dressing room elaborately decorated in all-natural rich woods, built-in closets, and full-length mirrors. Next is a spacious marble bathroom with one of the nicest and largest showers that I've ever seen in Southeast Asia, including one of those incredible rainfall showerheads. The tub is encased in marble at the far end of the room with red and pink rose petals leading the way from the entrance to the exit of the bathroom. More rose petals are sprinkled all around the bathtub where luxurious soaps, salts, bath foams, and other essentials are displayed for the perfect bathing experience. We exit left into the master bedroom where feather beds and pillows with Egyptian cotton sheets and duvets are there to wrap me in opulence.

Again, rose petals lead the way like crumbs from Hansel and Gretel, advancing me from one luxurious experience to the next round of opulence. Chocolates are placed on the pillows with care. At last, the tour is complete, and we return to the living room. Has Prince Charming come? I glanced in the mirror at myself; I suddenly realize I'm not prepared

for this. I'm fresh from the jungle, not befitting a Prince Charming yet or this Ritz-Carlton suite. I see that the girls are about to excuse themselves, and I grab them by their arms, "Girls, please, you have to help me. I need a manicure, pedicure, and a hair appointment cepat, cepat …" I need them quickly, quickly. "Can you help me on such short notice?" I say with panic sinking in.

With big smiles, the girls say, "Of course, Mr. Ron thought you might feel this way. It's all arranged, and they are awaiting your arrival at the salon." I remember how I had balked at Ron earlier on his offer.

"But first, Ms. Satrece, please sit down and enjoy your lunch and cocktail and admire your room. Ms. Safi will be ready to escort you to the salon whenever you are ready. No rush, enjoy your room first." And with that, they disappear.

Left standing alone in the middle of the room and in silence other than the love songs playing in the background, I find my cell phone, walk to the sofa and sit, curling my legs up under me. I telephone Ron, "Well, I believe you have outdone yourself," Satrece says very softly.

"So do you like it? Are you pleased with the arrangements?" Ron asks with excitement.

"Are you kidding? I'm…absolutely…speechless," Satrece says, still awestruck.

As laughter and satisfaction boom through the phone line, I close my eyes and allow Ron's heartwarming laughter to sink all the way to my core and readily savor it for a moment.

"Where are you in the room? Are you enjoying a Cosmopolitan yet?"

"I've just sat down on the sofa and am still admiring your handiwork."

"Well, please, reach over, pour yourself a Cosmo and sip it while we talk," Ron says this as though he is sitting in the room and knows every intimate detail. I do as I'm instructed, pour the drink and take a sip.

"How much more work do you have to do today?" Ron asks.

"Work? I'm no longer interested in any more work today!"

Ron has sheer pleasure in his laughter, knowing he has done everything possible to make me forget about work, thus allowing me to enjoy the evening.

Satrece asks, "How many roses are there?"

distraction

"Three dozen. One dozen for each hour we were together the day we first met."

"We were together three hours that day? And you noted that?"

"Yes, of course. There isn't much I don't remember about that day."

"Three dozen roses, huh?" Satrece smiles.

"Have you read your card or opened your gift yet?"

"No. I would rather wait until you are here."

"Well, that's sweet and thoughtful. But I really must insist that you open the gift now; it's something that you can enjoy this afternoon."

Satrece takes hold of the gift bag and returns to her position on the sofa. While she's opening it, she says, "And by the way, thank you for the salon appointments; I do need them as you presumed." Yet another satisfying bout of laughter booms through. "Though I've lived in the jungle for a long time, I pride myself in knowing that I'm merely one day of beauty appointments away from wiping off the life of remote and adventurous living and donning chic civilization again. But as of now, I only have a few hours."

Ron says, "Well, Ms. Satrece, enjoy your cocktail and appointments. Is there anything else I can do for you? I am anxious to see you this evening."

"I have to admit something to you, Ron," Satrece says, "I hadn't really put as much thought and effort into this date as you have, and I feel a little bit ashamed at the moment. I have just been so…so… preoccupied with struggles and my brother. I now have a busy afternoon of catching up."

"I recognize that. I forgive you this time," Ron says with happiness emanating, thinking that he finally has her undivided attention.

I open the gift and see that it's an iPod, but my instinct tells me that it isn't just merely an iPod. Ron suggests that I turn it on, and I soon discover that there are more than nine thousand songs loaded; it's a treasure trove of music. I'd mentioned to Ron earlier that one of the things I miss most about the States is the music. I'd been in a time warp and knew nothing of the new artists or today's music and would have no idea where to begin being reintroduced. This gift is proof that Ron has actually listened to me; how special is that? This gift touches my soul, and once again, I'm left speechless.

"So should we still meet at 5:30 as planned?" I finally say.

"Yes, I will be there with my driver then. I suggest we have a drink in your suite, and I've made reservations for us for dinner. Does that work for you?"

"Sounds perfect. And, Ron, I am really looking forward to this evening," at last I can say with sincerity.

Several hours later, I'm finally back in the room, frantically attempting to turn Cinderella into the fairy princess. To my dismay, I had to call Ron from the salon to postpone the time for our date. Ron must have threatened the salon girls too; they nervously worked with the swift and steady pace of a tortoise. Ron, as always, patiently understood. He was already en route to the hotel when I phoned him, but he is also delayed due to traffic gridlock and caught in political demonstrations. He has not moved in twenty minutes. I know the route from the Shangri-La Hotel to where I am, at the Ritz. He must travel through the Selamat Datang Monument and roundabout, strategically located in the heart of Jakarta's main avenue with thousands and thousands of vehicles passing through the roundabout on a daily basis. It's the main place where most civic and political groups

hold their demonstrations, and these demonstrations are very impassioned and testy due to recent events. For once, the demonstrations work to my advantage; an uncontrollable delay in Ron getting to the hotel as the rioters pound and bang on all the cars, hoping to get the world's attention. Thank goodness! I had tremendous apprehension in calling Ron with the news that I'd be late, with all that I have put him through and all that he has done, the wait continues still. How much patience can this man muster?

Ignoring the temptation of losing myself in the fabulous steamy shower, alluring makeup applied at record speed, I now stand in front of the dressing mirror admonishing myself for the outfit I selected for the evening. Perfection, if I were a gypsy traipsing through Thailand or Bali, but not Prince Charming or suite suited. I've now gone through option one outfit, option two and stand in option three. Unacceptable, and time is ticking away. At least option three is an LBD; there's bound to be something creative I can do with a little black dress. Quickly, I accessorize with rhinestone bra straps, allowing them to modestly peak out. I tie a black silk scarf around my hips and scrunch up the dress. I add my Cartier jewelry and my most dangly ear-

rings, then glance at the vision in the mirror once more. Better. I take my thick, shiny, salon-styled hair, rake my fingers through it, messing it all up—twist, twist, wrap and clip, wah lah, a messy French twist is born. Nearly there, I apply some bright red lipstick and soufflé-tasting bronze gloss, the twelfth hour has arrived; ultimately the image looking back at me is now acceptable.

The phone rings, and it's Safi asking if I am ready for Ron; he is on his way. I look around the dressing room at the pile of clothes strewn about; I quickly grab them up and stuff them in my suitcase, closing the lid just as I hear "the knock" on my door. So much for my fussy, nitpicking neatness. I stand tall, straighten myself and approach the door.

Meanwhile, Ron arrives at the concierge level and meets Safi. Safi informs Ron that Ms. Satrece has not yet returned from her salon appointments and offers him a drink. Ron gladly accepts a bourbon on the rocks to calm his nerves as he continues to anxiously wait to reunite with Satrece.

After a while, "Safi, are you sure Satrece hasn't returned yet? She called and informed me she was

running late, but she should be back in her room by now."

"I'm sure, Mr. Ron. She has to walk past my desk to go to the elevators; I'll know when she's back. Would you like another drink?"

"Yes, the same please and with a glass of water too." And he waits.

Shortly thereafter, Ron insists Safi call and check to see if I am back in my room. Safi calls, hangs up and turns to Ron.

"Oh, Mr. Ron, I'm so sorry, she *is* in her room; I don't know how I missed her. Satrece is awaiting your arrival." Safi escorts Ron to Satrece's room. She stops about ten steps from the door. "Are you ready, Mr. Ron? You have to do the rest on your own."

Ron is apprehended by his own nervousness, as he inspects the door. The last ten steps resemble walking down "the green mile." His whole life is in front of him right now. If he feels this way about this woman, and Satrece is everything he imagines her to be, everything *has* to go right. For the last few weeks, he's been trying to determine what he'd say to her. How will he greet her? Will he give her a hug, kiss her on the cheek or simply take her hand? Ron's lived through every scenario in his head. He's never been

this nervous in his life; he's met with delegations of some of the most wealthy and powerful people in various countries around the world. But he is *so* nervous; maybe this is the most he's ever been. Ron reassures himself, so far everything has gone well, though, he looks and feels great. He's successful and intelligent. He's tall, slender, and well-built. He's confident; he's everything she could want. He then hears Safi continue, "It's all yours, Mr. Ron."

Ron looks at Safi like, "Oh my god, you're not coming in with me?"

"I hope you have a wonderful evening," Safi says as she spins on her heels and departs.

In the brief moments, I stare at the door after hearing the knock; I despair that Ron won't be as I remember him…nor will he be the gentleman I think he is. I reach for the door and open it slowly, not altogether sure of what I will expose, or what I will say or what I will do. There he stands in full stature and poise, bearing dignity and distinction, as dapper and stately as I remember him to be. His smile is stretched from ear to ear, his smile is dazzling me once again. As the perfect gentlemen, he awaits for me to invite him in. After we both gaze at each other

in joyous exuberance, the feeling of our two worlds colliding, smiles radiating from both, I say, "Please, come in."

"We meet again," Ron says; and without further hesitation, he steps in and places his hands on my hips while continuing to deeply gaze into my eyes. He then gives me a soft gentle kiss on my right cheek and takes both my hands into his.

I reply, "After all that's happened, how about a hug?" We hug each other warmly and graciously; I take Ron by the hand and lead him to the sofa. With all doubts and uncertainties evaporated, comfort and exhilaration seeps in for us both.

Ron says, "I found myself suddenly wondering as the door opened, if you were anything like I remembered. You are a stunning and elegant woman, every part of you as perfect as I remember."

It seems this man frequently leaves me speechless; I'm not sure how to reply to this. "I was also wondering if you were like I remembered…and you are."

I notice that Ron pauses long enough for his eyes to sweep the room; his every instruction has been executed flawlessly, and an expression of satisfaction flashes across his face.

"May I fix you a drink, a Cosmopolitan perhaps?" Ron asks.

"Yes, please. You obviously know the bar better than I do, so would you do the honors?" I chuckle.

Ron goes to the area where he has had the bar set up and calmly and skillfully begins mixing and shaking the cocktails. Soon, he returns with my Cosmo and his dirty martini, garnished artistically and serves our drinks suavely. I can't believe how confident and in control this man is. We drink a toast. "Cheers… to us meeting again and having the time to get to know each other."

We chatter about the events leading up to this juncture, including the riots that Ron just travelled through to get to my hotel and the reasons for my late return from the beauty salon. I inquire about all the items making up the bar. Ron hand-carried the crystal martini glasses, the silver skewers, and the stainless cocktail shaker from America. He purchased what ingredients he could in Jakarta, and the remainder, including the alcohol, was acquired in the Duty Free shops while traveling in and out of Singapore. These items would become gifts for me, which I will carry back to Jepara to remember this occasion.

Once again, I've found that Ron's attention to detail has left me flabbergasted. The worries I initially experienced when he asked me on this date, on this side of the world, could now be set aside. I had apprehension that I might be just another girl in another "port" for this man. I now witness the fine points he aligned to make this date extremely special and memorable. I don't think he is doing the same for other women in any other country.

Ron fixes us another round of drinks. The conversation never stalls, the laughter and smiles never stop, and the fascination never ceases. Ron is a tremendous amount of fun; he's charming, witty and wise with a towering intellect that is impressive. We gracefully maneuver topics across all interests and borders.

I finally ask, "What time is our dinner reservation?"

"I made them for seven-thirty."

"What time is it now?"

"It's…after…nine-thirty. My goodness, the time has flown. It's been three hours…again. Three hours seems to be our magical number."

"Do you need to call the restaurant?"

"No," Ron smiles and says with certainty. "They know we're coming."

"Where is it that we're going?"

"We are going to the Dharmawangsa Hotel, to its restaurant, Sriwijaya. Are you familiar with it?"

"Yes, it's my favorite restaurant in all of Jakarta! How *did* you waltz in here and find the best hotel and the best restaurant in town? You are *good*! You're really good!"

Ron smiles again with certitude. "Shall we go now?"

"Yes, absolutely. Suddenly, I'm famished."

"I'll call my driver and let him know we're on our way down. How long do you suspect it will take us to get there?"

"In these riots and traffic, forty-five minutes at best. In the absence of traffic, if that were possible here in Jakarta, it would take less than fifteen minutes."

As we enter the grounds of the hotel for dinner, a peaceful and prestigious oasis of serenity with timeless architectural design surrounds us. Ron and I saunter hand in hand to the Sriwijaya, lost in conversation. I know that it must be getting close to closing time for the restaurant since it's Wednesday evening. Upon our entrance, I hear, "Mr. Ron and Ms. Satrece, welcome! Your table awaits you. I hope you

enjoy your evening," says the hostess as she shows us to our table.

As we approach our table, I once again stop dead in my tracks. I see red roses and lots of them on our perfectly selected table. I see pink and red rose petals sprinkled around; the tabletop is appointed with many lit candles and more chilled champagne. I see our waitress standing close by at attention dressed in a tuxedo with a white cloth draped over her arm. Nobody seems to care that closing time is only thirty minutes away. As Ron pulls my chair out for me, I notice that we've been placed where it seems that we are the only guests in the restaurant. Has Ron reserved the entire restaurant for us?!

"Let me guess…would these be three dozen red roses by any chance?" I ask smiling.

"Yes, it is. How did you ever guess?" Ron replies with his same smugness and smile.

"Do you think that *maybe six* dozen red roses in one day is a little…excessive?" I ask, trying to hold back laughter.

"For you, definitely not. I'd love to surround you in red roses every day. Would you like some champagne?"

"Certainly. I see you did it again."

"Did what, again?"

"Plan every precise detail in advance. Do the people here hold the same fear of you as the staff did at the Ritz?

Ron looks around smiling, "No, I don't see any fear anywhere. I only see people that want to serve and please you," Ron says as the cork pops off the champagne.

"May I make the toast this time?" Satrece offers.

"Yes, please do, I would like that."

"To the most memorable evening of my life and to the most endearing and enchanting gentleman I have ever met to share it with."

As Ron becomes lost staring at Satrece for the moment, he realizes the serendipity bestowed upon him is nothing short of a destined love, a karmic connection. His love for this woman has already ascended through the ranks at a pace that bewilders him. Her radiance illuminates an entire room; her infectious smile warms the hearts of everyone nearby. She is beautiful and tall like a model; he can see her eyes looking up as if from pages of a magazine, and she makes him feel like he can do and accomplish anything. He could just soar; Ron thinks

he can conquer the world with her at his side. He aches to kiss her, so he leans in.

I see Ron leaning forward as though he wants to whisper into my ear. As I too lean into Ron, without wavering, he kisses me with a sweet tender reverence. I'm rather surprised, so I yank back immediately. I see the warmth and affection in his eyes; then I consider that I actually enjoyed his kiss, as a matter of fact, I genuinely fancied it. I find myself leaning back in to complete the "first kiss."

As we both lean back and dreamily open our eyes, Ron says, "I have been waiting for that kiss for a very long time."

How is it that this man always leaves me in a shortage of words? Any witty responses continue to bail on me. I reach for my champagne to save myself, and it seems the cat's got my tongue again.

Ron asks about dinner and what I'd like to start with. I order escargot and a salad, highlighting beets and goat cheese. Ron orders the same. We nibble at the starters and finish the champagne. Ron requests a wine list from the waiter, and he asks me if I prefer red or white.

Thinking that I don't need any more alcohol, but neither do I want the night to end, I suggest red.

distraction

"What are you going to order for your entrée?" I inquire.

"Whatever you have, I'll have the same."

"No, don't do that to me. This is the most delectable restaurant in Jakarta, order something *you* will truly enjoy. I like to be experimental."

"Whatever you're having is perfect for me. Really, Satrece, I'm not hungry; all I desire is to be close to you."

The rapture persists while we're lost in intoxicating conversation. The waitress approaches Ron and whispers something into his ear. Ron, somewhat amazed, tells me that it is nearing two in the morning, and that the chef would like for us to order, so he can close the kitchen for the night; the restaurant has been closed for hours. However, they have enjoyed witnessing our romance blossom, so once we order, we can take all the time we like. There's that magical three hours again. I order the halibut en papillote covered with a dill and thyme cream sauce served with truffles and asparagus tips. The artistic presentation of colorful sauces delicately spooned and dotted on the plate is as exquisite as the meal is. Ron responds with, "I'll have what she's having." I'm

famished and eat my entire meal while Ron pushes
his meal around his plate and only takes a few bites.

With it being the wee hours of the morning,
and unfortunately no traffic at this time, the route
back to the Ritz only takes about ten minutes. It is
the first time that I'd ever *wished* for traffic in Jakarta.
Ron escorts me up to my room and is standing at the
floor-to-ceiling windows looking out over the city
lights. "It's not long before sunrise," he sighs. "I must
apologize for keeping you out so late, that was never
my intention. I'm not sure how it happened. I admit,
I still don't want this night to end." The unhappiness,
which glooms from his face, mirrors the unhappiness in my heart.

"I don't want the night to end either. Nor am I
certain how it happened; it's been a marvelous evening, and it's just flown by."

"Well, I think it's time for me to go." Ron envelopes me in his arms and gives me a kiss with passionate affection and desire. He then takes both of my
hands into his and says, "Good night, sweetheart."

"Maybe you don't…*have*…to go …"

"What do you mean?"

"Maybe it would be nice for you to hold me tonight, to feel your arms wrapped around me while I sleep."

"Are you sure? Are you *really* sure?"

"Yes, it's nearly morning. I would hate for you to have to cross town at this hour and possibly get caught in the demonstrations starting back up."

"I would like that very much." Without faltering, Ron leads me by my hand to the master bedroom. The turn-down service has pulled the covers back and delivered the copious amount of pillows I always sleep with. Ron unbuttons his shirt and throws it on the bed. I take his shirt, put it on and wiggle out of my dress, unclip my hair and kick off my high heels. He sits down on the bed and takes his shoes and socks off, stands and steps out of his slacks. I feel the panic pulsating through myself, thinking, *was this a good idea after all?* Did he understand what I meant? I notice his adorable Ralph Lauren boxer shorts in navy, white and black stripes; it makes me smile inside. I see his broad shoulders, his V-shaped waist, and his well-built legs. He motions for me to enter into the bed. I crawl in, arrange and fluff all the pillows, and lie on my side to watch him enter. Ron slides into bed and puts his arm lovingly around my

shoulders; I put my arm around his chest and further snuggle my head into his neck; it occurs to me how much I like this place. He reaches with his other hand and strokes my arm and kisses my forehead. I'm in heaven and am quickly asleep.

I feel the rustling of covers, and I sense a change. I peek out of one eye, only to find Ron awake, with his head resting on one of his arms staring at me with a huge boyish smile. The smile says, "Come out, come out and play with me."

"Aaahhh, you're awake already?" Satrece moans.

"It's after seven-thirty, it's late for me."

"But we only just went to sleep; my brain's still fuzzy, I need more rest," Satrece pouts.

"Darling, if you need more sleep, then that's what we'll do. I'll take any excuse to hold you close to me longer."

I roll over on my side, and he spoons me with his arm around me. Ron has been true to this word; he has been cavalier in not doing anything to make me feel the least bit pressured or uncomfortable. *All in due time, nice and slow,* I think as I drift into slumber once more.

After a few more hours, we awake, and I order coffee for two. Attired in our plush robes, we lie in

bed and drink our coffee. I order brunch for us: two large trays are delivered, so we crawl back into bed and leisurely consume our lovely meal. Ron isn't so keen on our healthy fare of the eggs Florentine and turkey bacon, so he grins and asks, "Where are the side orders of pancakes, hash browns, and sausage?"

We find ourselves standing at the massive windows staring down at the city of Jakarta. "If you had a choice, would you live in Jakarta or Singapore?" Ron asks.

"Singapore, without a doubt. Why do you ask?" Ron hesitates, and before he speaks again, I urge, "Tell me more about you and your job."

"My job is boring. I'd rather talk about you."

"If you don't tell me what you do, I'm going to assume you are a…a drug dealer or something and have something to hide," I state adamantly.

Without hesitation, Ron reaches for a pen and a cocktail napkin on the nearby coffee table and immediately starts sketching on the napkin. "In the oil and gas industry, the business is divided into upstream and downstream. I work in the upstream side …" For the next two hours, Ron draws and explains while I inquire; six napkins later, I have a notable understanding of Ron's business.

"So, does this prove to you that I'm not a drug dealer?"

Both of us laugh heartily.

Now that I have Ron's undivided attention, I further inquire about his daughters and family. Ron's father died when he was a young boy; he was raised in North Dakota by his mother and older sister when his mother was absent. He shares with me about his sister Staci and how she has influenced his life, and that there could not be a more lovely and generous person in the world. Ron reveals to me how close he is to *all* of his "girls."

"Ahhhh, that explains it...you and *your girls*. That's why you've been so perceptive about things such as my makeup and nail polish, and it further explains why you're such a gentleman."

"You think I'm a gentleman?"

"Yeahh, the perfect gentleman."

Ron smiles and says, "I'm not sure if I'm such a gentleman to everyone else, but anyway, now that I've survived your inquisition, it's my turn. Tell me more about your ex."

A frown overtakes my face. "There's not much to talk about...rather, nothing *I want* to talk about."

Ron isn't giving up, and with sheer resolve, eventually, he hears tales of lies, deceit, infidelities, abuses, abandonments, and every other god-awful thing you can think of.

Ron sits back and processes Satrece's brief accounts of past events along with what he's already discovered about her, and he suddenly realizes that now he fully gets her. He has become intimately conscious of her being, like having that crystal ball to delve into her heart, allowing him to see the unfolding dimensions and scars of her soul. Through one reason or another in her lifetime, she'd been abandoned or hurt by every person close to her starting with her parents and her father's premature death. It has been a lifetime of sorrow and pain that led her to build twelve-foot walls that surround her heart. He can appreciate her bravery, her strength and independence, and especially her determination and stubbornness, and much more. If Satrece only knew how he ached to hold her in his arms and to promise her that he'll protect her for the rest of his life. If she only knew, if she would only LET him. Ron instinctively knows that if he isn't careful or moves too quickly, he'll see just how quickly she can, and will, run away.

We decide to spend the afternoon as "if it were a normal day for me in Jakarta." I will take Ron to Da Vinci Furniture to see the exquisite luxury furniture from the finest manufacturers around the world,

a one-stop shop for me to investigate and scruti-
nize my toughest competition. We will dine at C's
Restaurant in the Grand Hyatt, my second favorite
restaurant in town. The hostesses at C's always seat
me at my favorite table in an intimate corner overlooking the sophisticated open kitchen as the chefs
take center stage. I made our dinner reservatory,
and believe it or not, the evening didn't include three
dozen red roses, nor pre-chilled champagne awaiting
our arrival. But we still managed to have a lovely evening after all.

Ron suggests that since we both have spent so
much time in Jakarta that we go somewhere else for
the weekend. He suggests Singapore, and I accept.
As I shower, Ron makes our travel arrangements; we
plan to depart the next morning. We make our way
to the Shangri-La Hotel, so he can shower and pack
his bags.

I keep asking myself, *is this the right thing to do?*

18

Some Enchanted Evenings in Lands Far Away Singapore, 2008

s we sit aboard our short Singapore Airlines flight, we each revel at how adept and effortlessly we had packed, checked out of the hotel, checked in at the airport and made it onward through immigration together, like we had done it a million times together. We travel together like souls from the past. Ron fills out my embarkation card, mostly by memory, including my passport number, making me feel uneasy, already succumbing my independence. But no one has ever done this for me before, so…cool.

Arriving in Singapore, we disembark the plane, proceeding through Changi Airport as we each have done a hundred times before. We are discussing the things we love most about Singapore when I stop and realize that I have no idea where we are in the airport. We are two suave international business travelers, and we are strolling through the airport like two young inexperienced lovers. We had glided past *every* large EXIT and IMMIGRATION sign that's well placed throughout the terminal and stand staring at the end of the terminal wall.

Back on track now, I'm through immigration, and Ron hands his passport to the immigration officer. I ponder if all immigration people practice frowning in the mirror each morning, as I've never seen such a solemn bunch of people. It must be their mandate to make people scared; it's nearly impossible to get one to smile back at you. Suddenly, the immigration officer's face makes even a larger scowl as he barks, "What's this?"

"It's a smiley face from this beautiful woman. There's a romantic story behind it," Ron informs the official with a boyish smile.

I see it's the same smiley face that I'd placed in my passport when I sent it to Ron in Jakarta.

"Really?" The officer eyes me as I smile meekly and shake my head.

He looks back at Ron, "I love romantic stories. Welcome. Have fun in Singapore!"

I'll be doggone. Did that really just happen? And the immigration officer actually gave us a congenial smile? He loves romance?

Entering the taxi, I speak to the driver, specifying our destination. Ron quickly informs me that it's his job as the gentleman to speak to the taxi driver. Hmmm…says who? I muse.

"Oh no. I forgot to change money; I don't have any Sing dollars to pay the driver," Ron moans.

"It's okay, I've got you covered on this one. I have some." Satrece smiles.

"I can't believe I forgot to change money," Ron says somewhat to himself chuckling. "You do really distract me. I'll pay you back as soon as we find a money changer."

"Don't be ridiculous, that's not necessary. Let me get this at least," Satrece says, challenging Ron.

Ron instinctively knows not to challenge Satrece back just now.

The taxi pulls up to The Ritz-Carlton, Millenia Singapore overlooking Marina Bay. The Ritz has

worked for us so far, so why change now? We maneuver our way to the reception desk, through the lobby filled with contemporary art and a grand piano, and proceed with check-in. The reception clerk immediately recognizes our names.

"You are the guests visiting us from our sister hotel in Jakarta! Welcome to the Millenia Singapore! We've heard all about you, and we have a lovely room prepared for your stay. We hope your stay is as romantic here as it was in Jakarta."

As I blush, Ron beams proudly, "Yes, we *are* your special guests." I notice the entire staff behind the desk glance up at us and smile; they start whispering amongst themselves as they continue to eye us. I prefer to carry on life as incognito as possible, more than enough attention seems to get diverted my way, but Ron, on the other hand, perks up like a peacock parading his feathers in grandeur. Good grief.

We're shown to our room, a junior suite overlooking the sparkling azure bay, Singapore River, and the city skyline. The room, of course, is complete with three dozen red roses, pink and red rose petals sprinkled about, chocolates and fruit, and two large towels cleverly folded into two swans kissing, cre-

ating a large heart upon the bed. Why am I aghast again? How many times can this guy keep doing this?

We both walk over to look out of the expansive windows on the twenty-third floor; again, Ron takes my hand in his and holds it as we enjoy the breathtaking views. I'm thinking how this is beginning to make me feel uncomfortable, always grabbing my hand. I like my space.

Abruptly, unexpectedly, images of six F-16 Air Force jets race close by just before our eyes, displaying an aerobatic demonstration of precision and maneuverability at our window. We stand hand in hand in reverence and admiration as the team moves in nimble and strategic directions with adrenalin-pumping spins, rolls, and loops. The F-16s, then in full splendor, maneuver expertly while releasing smoke, spell out the word "LOVE" across the sky. As Ron and I look at each other and blink in amazement, we turn back to the windows in time to see a large heart of smoke paint the sky. As though that wasn't enough, another jet speeds through the heart, making a line as if it were shot with an arrow. I hold Ron's hand as tightly as he is holding mine as we watch the rest of the remarkable exhibition. As chills travel all through

my body, a thrill fills my heart. Was this really fate slapping me upside the head?

"Did…you…are you…responsible …" Satrece stutters.

"I wished I could take responsibility for this, but I don't know the Prime Minister of Singapore, and I didn't order the F-16 exhibition…I wished I'd thought of it though." Ron laughs haughtily.

I acknowledge to myself for the first time, I have to give this weekend a real chance, but a chance for what? Is there such a thing as *true love*? Does anybody really fall in love anymore? No, I don't think so. But "LOVE" just appeared to us in the sky, along with a great big heart shot by cupid. And now, *maybe it seems,* fate had tried to appear to me in the DFW Airport, and maybe again in Jakarta. Something to definitely ponder.

The bell captain delivers our luggage and says, "I see you are enjoying our Black Knights aerobatic team. They are rehearsing for our upcoming National Day where the Prime Minister will speak on love, compassion, determination, and unity."

Ron asks, "What would you like to do, Satrece?"

"Keeping in my tradition, I'd like to take you to one of my favorite places I enjoy after arriving

in Singapore. Are you familiar with the iconic hotel, Raffles? There's a quaint Colonial cocktail bar with a white gazebo set in tropical palms and indigenous plants including fountains, birds, music ..."

"Raffles Courtyard, yes, it's one of *my* favorite places! That's where *I* was going to suggest we go. We'll unpack later, come on, let's go."

As we arrive at the Raffles Hotel, the exhilaration of the place lavishes us as it does each person that enters the grounds. "Perhaps the world's greatest hotel, not just a hotel, but an icon. Raffles Singapore stands where it has always stood, at the crossroads of civilization and culture, a Colonial oasis, calm and charm in the heart of modern Singapore—exclusive, historic, and one of a kind. Where the legend began and is enchanting and loved by those with an adventurous spirit and a taste for the very best," says its literature, and we fully concur.

Some enchanted evenings occur in lands far away as we sip our white wine and talk about this fabulous world. For dinner, Ron ushers me to one of his favorite little secrets, the Banana Leaf Apolo. We feast on traditional Indian food in a small casual setting in Little India. Northern and Southern fare served up simply yet delectably on an actual banana

leaf with its authentic aromatic spices creating an extravaganza of flavors. Ron drinks the local Tiger Beer, and I drink a specialty rose-infused lassi. We eat and nibble until we wobble back to the hotel for yet another night of loving snuggles and cuddles.

As morning arrives, we discuss what we want to do today in Singapore.

"One day, I would really enjoy the luxury of relaxing and frolicking at the beautiful swimming pool here," Satrece says.

"Then that's what we'll do today."

As I don my bikini, grab my sarong, book, and suntan oil, I'm ready to go in minutes, while Ron is still fussing over packing a swim bag. We enter the pool area, and my high spirits elate even more. Ron leads the way to two chairs underneath an umbrella in the shade, "How's this?"

As I gawk at him and look questioningly, I walk over to two chairs center staged in the sun with an umbrella close by. "I'm thinking these are much better," I say with my most appealing and convincing smile.

"What was I thinking? Of course those are the perfect set," Ron chuckles.

I quickly have my chair adjusted, towels rolled out, oil applied and am stretching and reclining allowing the vitamin D to soak in. I watch as Ron dons a hat, then applies face cream, the sport 30 sunscreen comes out; he applies it then asks me to apply it on his back. Ron adjusts his chair and then readjusts his chair. He adjusts his towels then readjusts his towels. He readjusts his hat and finally sits back. Within minutes, his left foot is bouncing all around like keeping time to music that isn't there.

Hmmm, the first thing in which we aren't totally aligned. I see my date isn't a big lover of relaxing poolside. I reach over and place my hand on his leg. "Is there something bothering you?"

"No. Why would you ask that?"

"That dancing foot of yours tells me you aren't too practiced in relaxing."

Ron looks down at his foot. "Oh, I'm sorry." He laughs. "No, I don't relax too often."

Before he knows what's happening, I jump up and am standing by the side of the pool. "The last one in is a turkey, I'll race you to the other side!" I say as I dive in.

If he doesn't know how to relax, I'll wear him out. I start swimming the distance at a comfortable

Satrece

pace, knowing I left Ron far behind. A mammoth splash overtakes me in the pool, and I sense a hefty presence gaining on me swiftly. Ah, a little competitive is he? If he's up for it, the contest is on! We're now racing to the other end of the pool, each of us swimming to win.

As Ron touches the side of the pool, he comments, "It's remarkable how you glide through the water like you're half fish."

"You're awfully strong yourself, but you remind me more of a bull thrashing through the water," I tease. "Come on, again!" I say as I kick off from the side and swim away. Head start or not, he's determined to not allow me to get away. We arrive at the other end, and I am off again as soon as Ron touches.

Back at the other end, we are both breathing hard and having a good laugh. Unexpectedly, Ron grabs me in his arms and holds me like he is about to carry me across the threshold, still in his arms, then Ron sets out to walk the length of the pool. With my arm around his neck, we are face to face and boob to face. "Now these are my kind of laps," Ron says, "I think I will call these the Ron & Satrece laps."

Ron is now relaxed and carefree. We spend the rest of the day frolicking and playing, doing regular

laps, gobs of Ron & Satrece laps, and soaking in the golden rays.

Back in our room and still in our swimsuits, we walk to the windows hoping to see more F-16 jets make hearts at our windows, but no such luck this time. With inscrutable lore, Ron further questions me on more details of my life before Indonesia, including my first career. Ron is fascinated with my early successes and proud of my achievements in the software industry. Though Ron seems to understand me well, my life is still an enigma to him.

I further inquire how it came about for him to live in and manage Indonesia and then West Africa. I'm equally enticed and fascinated about his career accomplishments.

We've been sitting cross-legged on the floor in front of the windows for hours now. We decide to take our showers and are both swathed in our plush bathrobes, not sure what our evening plans include since we had dined poolside only a few hours earlier. With my hair still wet hanging down my back and very little makeup on, Ron leads me to the love seat.

"There is something I want you to listen to." He gets his iPod and gives me one ear bud, and he places the other in his ear and plays a song. Ron listens and

smiles as he reflects on the words. I fumble with my large earpiece trying to keep it in; it falls out over and over, and now I am holding it in my ear. I've missed most of the song, but I realize it's an old song, something romantic. I've lost interest; the song ends.

"What did you think?"

"Uh…it's nice."

"Do you even know what it said?" Ron chided.

Dang it, I'm caught. "Not really, the ear bud is too big for my ear."

"Well, get *your* ear buds, and we'll listen to it again, listen closely this time."

Aduh or ouch, I've been reprimanded. I do as I am told, and the song begins:

> *Some enchanted evening, you may see a stranger …*
> *Across a crowded room.*
> *And somehow you know, you know even then,*
> *That somewhere you'll see her again and again.*
> *Who can explain it?*
> *Who can tell you why?*
> *Some enchanted evening, when you find your true love,*

When you feel her call you, across a crowded
room.
Then fly to her side. And make her your
own,
Once you have found her, never let her go …

OMG, he is so much more romantic than me.
"It's nice…romantic …"

"Ever since I saw you across the room in the
airport, this song has echoed through my mind. Isn't
it just perfect?"

I just look at Ron and smile; how do I answer
this? I have no idea. "Let me play you one of my
favorite songs by Wendy Slaten …" I quip and start
my song:

Nobody knows the hurt that
I hide
Nobody knows what I am feeling
inside
Everybody sees the me, I choose to
show
Nobody knows, nobody knows.
One by one everybody leaves

Ain't nobody tough enough to let
me be me
Everybody goes, everybody goes.
And there ain't nobody to count
on when I lose my way
And there ain't nowhere to lean
at the closing of the day ..."

"Stop it! Enough of this song," Ron snaps.

Aduh, reprimanded twice! I mumble, "Well, it does sum up my life pretty nicely."

Ron gazes into my eyes, "Darling, now that I have found you, I'm never going to let you go. I plan to always be here for you. Don't you understand that?"

Yeah, right. What about the minor little fact you live thirteen thousand miles away from me, on the other side of the world. Not to mention we've only spent four entire days together, is ringing through my mind.

Ron takes my face in his hands as if he's found his utmost treasure and kisses me with a masculine hunger yet sheltered by his gentle manner. He stops to admire and reassure me, yet looks into my eyes and kisses me again. I feel the singular warm embrace of his lips on mine; they are electric and luscious, and

distraction

I know something within us is changing, driving our thirst, one for the other. I feel his passion growing; he kisses me with a fervor that I cannot turn away from. He has been only a perfect gentleman thus far; I feel locked in his spell, and I am letting go and enjoying his kiss. I relinquish all the thoughts racing through my brain and allow Ron's passionate kisses to transcend to my lips and into my body. He pulls me close to him and wraps his arms tightly around me.

I catch Ron's eye as he peers into mine. A warmth and passion is rising between us; I feel as if a galaxy of passion and erogenous desire envelops me. He is standing at the door of my heart, and I feel his knocking at my sanctuary of femininity.

My longing and desire is awakened by my feel of him; he is rock hard and raring himself through my very core, just like a stallion. And as if the heavens obey our will, the final sunlight floods across me in Ron's arms and relinquishes the sky to the rising silvery moon; I am covered by its glow and shimmer. My heart is pounding beneath my flesh, and our kisses grow more and more desirous. Ron slides his arms under me, picks me up from the love seat and carries me to the king-sized bed with the over-

285

sized pillows and the rose petals he sprinkled upon it. He lays me down; half of his body is pressed atop mine, and our legs are intertwined. After kissing me more, Ron slides his right hand inside my robe and caresses my left breast, and my body starts to ascend to a sweet surrender. His face fills my view, and he is perfect to me. He unties my robe and opens it. He looks lovingly at my body; the smile that stretches across his face tells me he approves.

His eyes are filled with the nakedness of me, and he cannot hide his astonishment with the revelation that I am entirely hairless. I see and feel his excitement and intensity swell. His right hand is drawn again to fondle my left breast and twizzles my nipple that extends as he gathers it from the top with his right thumb and forefinger. He bunches the flesh of my breast and plumps it as I feel the warmth suffusing in my bosom. I can't keep quiet. His hand relinquishes my breast and moves to caress my flat tummy and tight, swelling thighs with gracious tender, long, slow strokes. His head falls into my right breast, and he nuzzles the nipple now with his lips, as it grows to meet his tongue and hardens into a pink bud. He nuzzles his face in the middle of my breasts. He kisses and fondles them more with

his tongue. He takes his sweet time as though he is savoring every ounce of pleasure they offer up to him. I arch my back and release my sexual soul to touch his. My breasts are plump and firm, as he bites at my nipples more, moving my breasts firmly so as to feel their weight. Ron's desire is hard and almost painful to him, and is now urging him to take me almost mercilessly.

He mounts me, parting my legs. He gives the inner flesh of my thigh a soft pinch, a most gentle pinch, and clasps my right breast in his left hand, as he slides himself inside me. I can feel him holding me up as he gathers my mouth to his. He breaks through my longstanding innocence that I've held onto thus far. He sucks on my lips as if to draw my very life and sexual desire inside himself, and I feel his seed explode within me as I reach my climax simultaneous with his, and together, we cry out inside the arms of one another, staring into each other's eyes. I can feel myself ascend and soar toward heaven, and quietly I linger in an afterglow of postcoital bliss. Together we hold onto one another and shudder and quake as our bodies simmer. It is at this moment that I know I've opened a door I cannot go back through; I've crossed the threshold to what can only cause us tre-

mendous pain and anguish in the days to come when we are no longer together. But my lust is drawn to his; what have I begun?

We awake the next morning to repeat much of the same as the night before. As we slowly and unwillingly separate our entangled bodies, a glow permeates our faces, and smiles radiate from our hearts.

We decide to spend the day wandering the infamous Orchard Road. It's a swanky boulevard with distinctive shopping malls, restaurants, and hotels, perhaps comparable to Fifth Avenue in New York but in a Southeast Asian environment. It is described as the "shopping belt that offers nearly 800,000 square meters of retail, dining, and entertainment options to please any taste or budget—from opulent brands to high street fashion. Outside of the malls, the main thoroughfare is immaculately landscaped with flowers and greenery, creating pockets of cool, natural calm amidst the hectic urban sprawl."

The people come from all across the region from places like China, India, and Southeast Asia to shop on Orchard Road. Shopping isn't our agenda, but there are a few things I need to pick up. We pass by one designer boutique after another with Ron

repeatedly saying, "Wouldn't this dress look sexy on you…and that one?" I can see the raw hunger in Ron's eyes now that he has undressed me and redressed me a myriad of times today. I smile inwardly and drag him onward. He shuffles me into numerous shoe boutiques, not taking no for an answer, Ron suggests various stilettos that I model for him. I'm sure many women would love to model high-dollar designer shoes, but I just can't envision them in the jungle or walking through the factory. I imagine that he sees my legs, and these heels wrapped around his neck; I can't help but ask myself, *does he have a foot fetish, shoe fetish or both?* I notice one thing all the shoes have in common, at *least* four-inch spiked high heels or higher; certainly he doesn't expect anyone to WALK in these shoes!

We find ourselves at the Crossroads Café, another of "both our favorite places." It's a Marriott bistro sitting on the corner of Orchard Road and Scotts Road, a café where East meets West and a casual and cozy place for premier people watching. We have a bottle of Cakebread Chardonnay while nibbling and finger feeding each other their signature hors d'oeuvres.

Once back at the hotel, Ron suggests we have a martini in the lobby lounge. Ron meticulously chooses the perfect seating, confirms that I'd enjoy a Cosmo and waves for the waiter. He waits for our beverages to be delivered, which are served in an unorthodox martini glass with squiggly colored stems; very fetching. Ron seems a little anxious to me; without explanation, he stands and walks to the black lacquer grand piano nearby, takes a swig of his martini and places it and his napkin on top of the piano. Ron sits down at the keyboard, and the "Chariots of Fire" theme song booms from the grand piano as Ron's hands dance across the keys. Stunned and in awe of this man, I humbly sip my Cosmo as he serenades me. He follows that with "Fur Elise." If a woman were to make a list of the top qualities of a desirable man, I'd have checked all of them by now, maybe. Ron takes a pause, I smile at him for encouragement, and he begins playing "Lean on Me." Yes, absolutely, I'd have checked ALL the top qualities that define a great man by now!

Back in the room, just as I think I love every-thing about this man, he has yet another surprise for me; however, I learn quickly that I don't neces-sarily like all surprises. As we are freshening up and

"changing into something a little more sexy," Ron takes my hands and looks me in the eyes, "I love you, Satrece," Ron smiles tenderly and says so sweetly.

That !#@!&#%@# cat's got my tongue again! I stand frozen with no response whatsoever. Can someone really love you in five days? Is it possible? I can't fall in love in five days. Can I even fully, unconditionally, love?

Ron changes the subject, swiftly taking me off the spot, but the words are out there. Our soon-to-be hot night pauses in the awkwardness of the moment, but before long, my desires and body cease control of my mind, and I'm daringly seduced back to this man like the illicit and tabooed, forbidden fruit.

By morning, I pretend the awkward affirmation of love the night before never happened. We start the next day with a view of Singapore's magnificent cityscape from the Singapore Flyer, the largest Ferris wheel outside of the United States. We then hang out on Clarke Quay in the afternoon and into the evening, a historical riverside quay full of flare, cuisines and beverages from around the world. The end of this fantasy is lurking in both of our minds, and reality keeps peaking its ugly head around the corner. We've had nearly a week together with laughter

from the belly and smiles from the heart. A week I will never forget. I *cannot* fathom having to say good-bye and farewell to this man in the Jakarta Airport. I haven't had one phone call from the factory, which is extremely odd, but no news is good news, I assume. I haven't heard from David either, so everything seems under control. I ask Ron if we can spend the last night in Jakarta, so we can have a befitting departure from each other. He quickly sees the value in this and calls Yuti at the Pacific Place for a reservation as well as for the concierge to change our airline tickets. Ron asks if I would be willing to meet a colleague of his for breakfast before we depart Singapore tomorrow morning. He thinks it would be wise for me to meet his friend to validate his character and the legitimacy of his business. I relish in the idea; it will make him more genuine, as if that's really needed.

Ron briefs me the next morning, "We'll be meeting the general manager of the Asia Pacific region, and his name is Paul Hey." A more serious look emerges on Ron's face as he shifts into a business mode. We enter the breakfast area of the Ritz Hotel at the same time as our guest arrives. Paul is a dapper-looking English gent maybe in his mid-to-late thirties. After we are seated and navigate through

introductions, the gentlemen stay in their comfort zone and segue right into business. I listen intently as they brilliantly and strategically discuss the intimate details of one project after another.

As quickly as Paul led into a business conversation, he pivots his train of thought and addresses me, "So you live in Jakarta? Is that where Ron said?"

I correct him, explaining where I do live, in the middle of what other Westerners would consider nowhere. Even if Paul understands the *where* better than most, he looks at me like a green-eyed monster as he tries to understand the *why.* The questions start flying. I compliantly answer each one, never offering more explanation than asked. I enjoy watching people's brains twist and turn as they weigh what to ask next; you can learn about a person that way. We finish the conversation with his unusual question, "What does a girl do for fun there, after so many years?"

Once I tell him that this girl traipses Southeast Asia with her yacht and crew, he turns to Ron and jokes, "Does she have a sister?" I guess that means I made the cut. Whew!

"No, she doesn't," Ron states proudly.

As Paul addresses Ron, "Now I understand why you requested the assignment here in Asia Pacific. Did you invite me to breakfast to raise the urgency of the request?" Paul asks.

It's all I can do to not spit my cappuccino across the table, as I sit up straight, my interest in their conversation having now tripled. Holy shit! Ron gives me a side-glance, smiling confidently, to observe my reaction after Paul surprised him with this question. Calmly, Ron responds, "I made the request before I met this beautiful woman, but since you brought it up, what is the status of my relocation?"

"Well, we really need you here, and there are many projects that would benefit from your knowledge and expertise. Your efforts just these last few weeks have made a significant difference for this team. But you know, it's about budgets and approval from Taylor that takes time, and *he* has to agree to this request."

Ron looks at me, "Steve Taylor is the president of our company. He involves himself with all expatriates' assignments."

I just nod my head like saying of course, as I'm still focused on regaining my composure.

"I would appreciate it, Paul, if you'd continue to work this issue for me," Ron urges.

Paul looks at me with a direct smile, "I will, buddy, I promise to see what I can do."

I've figured out that "buddy" is part of the international language of the oil and gas industry. There are a profuse amount of buddies in this fraternity.

We leave the restaurant later than anticipated and must hurry to board our flight.

Now calmly seated on board, I'm still processing the newly learned information with mixed emotions; he had already initiated a relocation? Wow, he could actually live in this region, or is it…Wow, not being forthright with this information is as good as lying to me.

Our flight is well on its way to Indonesia when Ron says, "You've been very quiet after learning my little secret this morning. Would you like to talk about it?"

I contemplate exactly what I want to voice, "Why and when did you request this new assignment?"

"I've planned for it a while now; I've wanted a change for a long time. My plan always was that after my girls were out of the house and married or established in their careers, I would request an over-

seas assignment again. I've waited patiently for a long time…trying to be the best father I can be. I put the request in about ten months ago before my youngest announced she was engaged and would be getting married."

"You requested Singapore?"

"Yes, or Europe, either place would be appealing to me."

"Why haven't you shared this with me?"

"I wanted to share this with you in Jakarta very badly, Satrece, the day after our first date. I had this feeling though that it would've scared you away. I thought it would be smarter with you to proceed slowly, with baby steps."

Run, baby, run! is exactly what my brain would've told me, but I didn't admit that to Ron. His behavior over the past months makes more sense to me now. Dating me would be a good fit into his long-term plans. But what about my long-term plans? One mesmerizing week doesn't mean we are compatible for the long run. If it seems too good to be true, it normally *is*.

"Is this the reason you asked me, 'If you had a choice, would you live in Jakarta or Singapore?'… And is either an option?"

"Yes, exactly."

"Do you think the relocation will happen?"

"Yes, I do. My company tries to take care of its people, and we have business around the world. But it won't happen until there is a direct need that can be monetarily or business justified. The worst thing that could happen if or when I do go overseas is that my career may not advance as much as I would hope, or I may miss a promotion."

"Why is that?"

Because the headquarters is in Houston, and that's where the executive leadership team needs to be.

"I see." I sit and ponder in silence as Ron gives me my space. "You know you have to make this decision exclusive of me, don't you?"

"What do you mean by that?"

"We've only just met, and your decision-making process must be based entirely on your own original motives." *Hmm, why do I get the feeling that just went in one ear and out the other?*

19

The Departure
and Good-bye

We arrive back at the Pacific Place in Jakarta; Yuti is able to get us our same room. She makes dinner reservations for us in the Ritz's premier restaurant. We commit to each other that we will enjoy every minute we have together, not letting the lurking doom and gloom ruin the last precious moments we have. The impending departure hovers, but we put our happy faces on as we freshen and dress for dinner.

Yuti has selected a table for us near massive windows overlooking the city skyline with views in front of us and to our left, leaving our backs to the other restaurant patrons. As we approach the table,

our host has a surprise for Ron and me—three dozen red roses await us and pink and red rose petals adorn the table with candle lights illuminating our entire corner, compliments of Yuti and the Ritz. How awesome! We are greeted by the chef, willing to make us anything for this special evening. With his suggestions, we order a premier bottle of wine paired with pecan-crusted lamb chops. We dine slowly, extending the evening as long as possible and savoring the masterful meal prepared for us, seemingly the most splendid dinner I'd ever had. For dessert, the entire restaurant staff presents us with a chocolate cake decorated with caramel and hearts, including our names artistically written. With our love and passion for Indonesia, along with our language skills, our kindness and our romance, many have come to wish us farewell and the best of luck in our blossoming love. They tell us they see the love all around us and how we make a beautiful, perfect couple.

The gracious smiles on our faces manage to keep the storms at bay.

We sleep very little that night. We make love and hold each other; we hold each other some more and make unselfish treasured love again. I love the scent of this man. We fit together perfectly when

we cuddle, and I adore the way he wraps me in his strong arms, holding me so closely.

The next morning, I shower and prepare to leave, as I have a six- to seven-hour trip home. Ron will check out later in the afternoon and move back to the Shangri-La Hotel; his vacation is concluded, but another two days of business has emerged. Nearly dressed and ready, I sense a transformation in the mood of the room, so I search for Ron. He's sitting on the sofa. To my alarm, the man I see sitting there doesn't resemble the man I've grown to admire and adore over the past week. *This* man sits with the weight of grief and despair on his shoulders, his vigor and love for life yanked from him. His jaw is dropped, his eyes are puffy and glassy, his color is pale; he looks like he's just lost his best friend. Instantly, I know that doom and gloom have just hit landfall. I sit down by Ron on the sofa; I take his hands in mine. "Ron, there's something I need for you to do for me. It's important to me. Will you do it?"

"Yes, my love, anything you ask. What can I do for you?"

"I need for you to be *strong* for me today. You have to do this for me. With us agreeing to meet each

other, it only meant that there would be good-byes and an end. I don't do good-byes; don't do this to me. Please be strong for us both. Please?"

Ron takes both of my hands in his and looks down for a lasting moment. He takes a few stabilizing breaths and looks up into my eyes. In a complete metamorphosis, a shine in his eyes overtakes the tears he concealed. His slack jaw is replaced by the smile I've so learned to love, and his stature and poise return to their full splendor. "My love, if you need for me to be strong today, so be it. I'll do anything for you."

An utter transformation has appeared before my very eyes. The inner strength that this man possesses leaves me struck in sheer admiration. I smile in amazement. "That's better. I'll put some uplifting music on…music soothes the soul. This is a playlist that I call My Happy Songs." We never discuss the unknown future or the next moment where we might or might not ever meet again.

Ron escorts me down to the driver, where some staff has gathered for support and to see me off. I pause to hold Ron, giving him a warm hug and breathing in his scent. I feel his arms around me one last time as we kiss good-bye. "Thank you for the

most unbelievable and amazing week of my life; I will *never* forget it."

"Thank you too. My darling Satrece, I love you. I love you so much."

I could only muster a sheepish smile and small nod; I turn and enter the car. I sink down into the seats of the Mercedes Coupe allowing them, needing them, to swathe around me. I never look back.

I never look back.

Ron watches the car drive away. As it nears the end of the driveway, the Mercedes is nearly out of sight before he turns away.

He can no longer bear to see the taillights or the silhouette of her head. His head drops to his hands; the tears can no longer be concealed. All of his strength has been ripped from him, his heart held in a vice grip. Pain and grief fill his entire body; his every muscle burns. Ron doesn't know if he'll ever smile again. Safi reaches up and puts her arm around his shoulders to console him; he begins to sob. Then the tears flow; he cannot stop them. He sobs and sobs some more. He has no control over these tears of sadness.

Returning to the room, Ron embraces her pillow; he can smell her provocative perfume. Her

distraction

laughter still fills his ears and his heart; her smile continues to penetrate his entire being. Sitting on the sofa, Ron recalls each and every moment and memory. No regrets. He had to see if she was everything he imagined. She was, she is. "My dearest Satrece, I will always love you."

20

Thailand, Here We Come!
2000

*T*ime is short-lived for the English couple from East Africa, Mick and Yavette, who I hired to help me with *Lady Satrece* and to work in the factory. As soon as I'm back home in Jepara from the maiden voyage of bringing *Lady Satrece* to Java, I suspect that I'm being taken advantage of and financially raped. I believe their plan is to milk all they can from this "pretty, sweet young lady" who's doing so well. I begin reconciling the monies spent on renovating *Lady Satrece*. I had been asking Mick for these receipts for months, but he continued to claim that he was too busy to get them in order. To my chagrin, I find there are tens of thousands

of dollars that are not reconcilable and unaccounted for.

I also learn from my staff that in my absence, Yavette stopped production of our customer's orders and produced every stick of furniture she desired for their home that we are building. She used business money to go to Jakarta for the weekend and bought every household appliance she wanted and had them shipped to Jepara, all while spending factory money. All of her new appliances far exceeded what I had, or what I decided to spend on myself, including a full-sized refrigerator and an oven with a stove.

I spend time until the wee hours of the morning, reconciling both Mick and Yavette's records. I'm now too pissed to sleep. I decide to keep them in the dark from my newest discovery until I have had time to further ponder this, cool down and gather more data. With a few phone calls to Singapore, I hear accounts of Mick being drunk from dawn to dusk, buying everyone living in the marina as much Tiger Beer as they wanted, as long as they would sit and chat with him. As I comb Yavette's receipts, I find gifts for her soon-to-be grandchild and her daughter-in-law. Enough is enough! Just because I'm a kind, giving and generous person doesn't mean that you

can take advantage of me, or that I'm a dumbass! I request a meeting with them at my home office and talk to each one individually, giving them a chance to defend themselves, to find more receipts or even to repay me for the abusive spending. I tell them both that I don't want to see their faces at the factory today, and they have twenty-four hours to appease me.

Just suffice it to say, the next morning when I met with each of them again, they were each independently *fired*! I put them on a plane to Jakarta the following morning. I receive three cheers from my staff and workers, but I'm out a freakin' bundle!

After many searches, failed efforts and horrible trial runs, I eventually find and hire a full-time captain, his name is Tito. He hires a first mate named Haris who is a foremost fishing authority, having won or placed in many fishing tournaments in Jakarta and Manado, Sulawesi. We have oodles of things to learn together, and they are a little leery of having a woman for a boss. There are so many new yachting and fishing terms I need to learn in Bahasa that it makes my head *spin*. I can hardly understand a thing they're saying, GJEESHK! Back to charades again. I teach the captain or "kapten" how to use all

distraction

the sophisticated electronic GPS radar chartplotter and autopilot systems. I then teach them the safety rules and regulations that we'll follow. Haris rigs all the fishing gear and outriggers to his specifications and begins to teach me how to use it. Haris or as called 'Aris by his friends teaches me how to tie all the proper boating knots.

I soon learn one of my biggest challenges is teaching the crew that *this* yacht or "kapal" will be well-maintained and kept clean like my home. *It is not going to look like a typical Indonesian fishing boat* with cigarette ashes spread around, the smell of fish with every breeze and unmaintained or salty equipment thrown about. It is *my home* while on the ocean. While the boat is docked, 'Aris takes the forward cabin as his sleeping quarters; the captain has the middle double berth, leaving the aft master cabin as mine, not to be used by others. If and when guests are on board, the crew will share the forward cabin.

After many one-day trial cruises, it's time for our first four-day test cruise to the Karimunjawa Islands, about eighty kilometers northwest of Jepara. It's Independence Day or "Hari Merdeka" for Indonesia, so we have a long weekend. The people at the factory are suddenly concerned with me being

on board a kapal with two other men, in such close quarters for four days. Hmmm, how to handle this? I recruit the assistance of Udin, an English-speaking supervisor from the factory, to accompany us on this trip. I need his help translating because many boating and fishing terms aren't in the dictionary, and he can act as my chaperone as well. Reluctantly, Udin agrees.

The Kap', 'Aris, and I have a great, fun and successful voyage. We work well together, learn a lot from each other, and we perfect our systems. We catch some fish, I do some diving, and we have a great time. Poor Udin is so sick; he is green and hanging over the side of the kapal the entire trip. Upon our return, he communicates to the people at the factory with authority that I *do not* and *will not* need a chaperone while aboard *Lady Satrece*. That was that.

As the year is coming to the end and the monsoons are around the corner, I decide it would be awesome to have *Lady Satrece* in Thailand for the season. Thailand is on the opposite side of the equator from Indonesia, meaning it will be sunny and in peak season there while we are in our monsoon season. Through this torrential rainy season, furniture production slows to a crawl, and my customers disappear for weeks at a time through the Christmas

and holiday season. So this year, I plan to spend the holidays on *Lady Satrece* in Southern Thailand cruising from island to island—another dream come true, and in the top five of my bucket list!

The crew is as *ecstatic* as I am for this voyage. I learn that for a true seafaring sailor, they smile their biggest while cruising at sea, no matter the family they're leaving behind.

I do research and determine that Thailand will not allow foreign boats to stay more than thirty days without posting a very large bond; however, the newly developing Langkawi, Malaysia nearby is trying to draw tourism by making itself a yachting haven. The laws for visiting boats and crew are very manageable and lenient.

I send the crew and *Lady Satrece* to Jakarta to get ready for the long voyage and to do the normal boat maintenance while I do an exploratory trip to Langkawi. I find the perfect home or marina for the season. The Royal Langkawi Yacht Club or RLYC is affordable, the Immigration and Customs is in walking distance from the marina, and the southern tip of Thailand is only a few hours away by boat. The Malaysian language is very similar to Bahasa, so the crew will be able to communicate and should feel

comfortable. It's still very sleepy here, but I believe someday it will be a major tourist destination.

Langkawi is an archipelago on Malaysia's north-western side known for its idyllic islets that are in the backdrop of the Andaman Sea. It offers an equatorial climate with tropical flora and fauna; it's an area of diverse mangroves, forests and rain forests, sandstone mountains, tidal flats, caves, and reefs, all of which coexist in harmony and abundance. This is a perfect short-term home for *Lady Satrece* and crew.

I make a resolution; I vow that *Lady Satrece* and its crew will *never* travel to a new destination without me. *CHARGE!* I will accompany and lead the way every nautical mile forward, allowing them to only backtrack without me. Having said this, I plan to send the boat and crew back to Nongsa Point Marina in Batam, where I will join them to check out of Immigration and Customs together and refuel. This allows me to work an additional week in the factory before I fly out to meet them. We will traverse the remainder of the journey together to Langkawi and onward to Thailand, culminating back in Langkawi where the crew will stand by.

The crew hires two additional crewmembers to help get *Lady Satrece* to Batam. Since I've done

the trip on her maiden voyage, we meet several times to give them every single detail they need to know. The chartplotter and paper charts have the route programmed and marked now, and the route is well documented. We understand our fuel and water consumption too. The transition season is here, so the weather should be perfect and without any surprises. I'm very pleased that the crew seems fearless about this trip; it's only later that I hear the "gossip" that if "Boss Lady" has already done the trip, they aren't about to show any fear or hesitation. Good boys, good crew.

I'm with them in Jakarta when they depart. We have checked, double-checked and triple-checked our list, supplies, plans and procedures. We are confident and prepared. They will depart after prayers the following morning, and I will fly home to Jepara. Once they are in Batam, I will meet them while they rest up for the next leg of the journey.

The first morning I'm home in Jepara, Captain Tito calls me from the satellite phone and tells me, "We have a problem." Oh no, this can't be good; I brace myself. The Kap' tells me that a cat was in a hatch and had babies, and none of us knew they were there. The mother cat must have scrambled off

when they started the engines, but now the boat and crew are about thirty hours out with four brand new baby kitties. "What are they supposed to do?"

Surely they aren't looking for my approval to throw them overboard. "Keep them alive and take care of them!"

"Apa?" (What?)

I repeat myself loud and clear and tell them that I will hold them personally responsible if *anything* happens to those kittens.

"Bagaimana?" (How?)

"Go ashore at Bangka and buy baby formula, buy a bottle of sambal, an Indonesia chili sauce, and empty the contents and use it as a bottle."

"Masa?!" (Really?!)

"Deliver the kapal to Batam *and* take care of the cats?" I can hear the disbelief in Captain Tito's voice.

"Tentu!" (Of course!) "Keep them alive for one week, and I will be there and figure it out." I know that Tito isn't too pleased with this conversation; in the end, he mumbles a lot of incomprehensible words and hangs up. I can only imagine what he just told me.

I arrive in Batam; *Lady Satrece* has been cleaned and looks great. The crew gets a good night's sleep, and I have four one-week-old kitties. What am I to

do with them? If I leave them in Batam, they will surely die. Looks like they are going to Thailand with me. Bottle-feeding the kitties every few hours is now part of *my* daily responsibilities, and seeing my dedication to the project appeased the crew that they had followed my orders.

The next leg of the trip will be onward to RLYC in Langkawi, Malaysia, approximately a three-day, two-night journey. Most of this leg is through the Strait of Malacca, which is a five hundred-mile stretch of water between the Malay Peninsula and the Indonesian island of Sumatra. From an economic and strategic standpoint, the strait is one of the most important shipping lanes in the world. It's the main shipping channel between the Indian Ocean and the Pacific Ocean, about one-third of the world's goods are carried through this channel. Piracy is and has been a major problem in the strait; there were about 220 attacks just last year alone. It is considered the third worst pirate grounds in the world. The directive information I've received for *this* strait is to Never, never, never! stop in the strait; these are the exact opposite instructions from the Bangka Strait where we were told to never travel at night.

Satrece

I'm so stimulated and vitalized to journey the Strait of Malacca that I can dance on water; I *must* have been a sailor in another life. The crew, who have their hesitations, can't let the lady boss show them off. Captain Tito is undoubtedly up for it, first mate 'Aris decides he wants the excitement, but the other two part-time hands are looking like frightened puppies. I give them an out: please do not do anything you aren't sure of. With that offer, one crew member hightails it out of there so fast he hardly waits for his salary. The other one decides to tough it out, being shown up by a woman just isn't cool. We—the Kap', 'Aris, a temporary hand, the baby kitties, and me— leave at sunrise the next morn.

No fears, mate, it was a piece of cake. Staying out of the way of the large ships and freighters during the dark nights had been our biggest challenge, thank goodness for satellite because the freighters come on fast. We near our marina, radio in and are led into our awaiting berth. We have successfully navigated the Strait of Malacca! My crew is feeling rather cocky and tough by now, and they are the envy of every other crew in the marina who spend their time leisurely cruising the local islands, never going too far.

distraction

The next morning, we clear Immigrations and Customs to enter Malaysia, send the extra crew member on his way home by plane, and the crew refuels while I buy more groceries and search for a Duty Free shop. The vacation officially begins now; some wine or spirits are definitely required. The kittens are about ten days old now, feeding them is getting easier, and their eyes have opened. They still live in the same hatch that they were born in.

I spend some time talking with the other yachtsman in the marina learning about all the "treasured gems" of Southern Thailand, the ones you can only see when you have your own yacht and get off the beaten track. They advise me to check in with Immigration and Customs for Thailand at Ao Chalong Yacht Club on Phuket. They also advise me to buy a "Phuket Sailing Guide," in which they are happy to mark all the special places.

"If I have to check in at Ao Chalong, am I allowed to visit all the other islands between here and there that you are telling me about?"

"Not officially, no."

"Well, uh…well …"

"But if you were to stop on these other islands, *unofficially*, to get food or supplies, we *suppose* that would be okay."

"Do you *unofficially* stop on the other islands to get food and supplies?"

"Of course...*unofficially*."

"What kind of trouble would I get in if I were caught, *unofficially* there?"

"You would be in *big* trouble."

"What is the likelihood of my *unofficial* stop being known?"

"Near impossible."

"Impossible?"

"There are ninety-nine islands in the Trang and Southern Phuket province, and I've never seen a single immigration officer on one of them."

"I see," but I don't see, I'm very confused, but I get the picture, I think.

I have a car CD player installed on *Lady Satrece* with six outdoor speakers mounted in all the right places. All I need now is to exchange some USD for Thai Baht, go into the main town of Kuah to buy some CDs, do the Duty Free shopping, and we'll be on our way. We have had two nights rest at the RLYC and are armed with good information; the crew is

as excited as I am. Duty Free doesn't have much to offer. Hmmm, there's lots of port wine, but I don't really drink anything else offered here. I've sipped port wine, but can it replace wine? I decide on five bottles of port wine. I remember that I will be able to buy the Thai's local Mekong whiskey along with ginger ale and a squeeze of lime; that will be my drink of choice again, but a variety is always good.

Thailand, here we come! With Christmas less than a week away, I decide not to spend too much time on the southern islands, also not to push my *unofficial* visits. We'll cruise by the islands that we want to explore more, look for future anchorages, and if need be, we'll stop to eat when we are hungry at the great inexpensive huts serving the awesome Thai cuisine. Why cook on the boat when the cuisine is so affordable and delicious?

The Kap' checks us out, and we are on our way. I put the new CDs into the player; unfortunately, I hadn't been able to find Christmas music, but I wasn't expecting to in a Muslim country anyway. I put in "Best Classics" and soon Gershwin's "Rhapsody in Blue" is booming from my speakers followed by Vivaldi's "The Four Seasons." I swear *Lady Satrece* and the waves are keeping time to the sophisticated

tunes from instrumental concertos; the visual of *Lady Satrece* and the waves is a waltz of absolute beauty! I then revel in the beauty of Langkawi with its dramatic mountain scapes, rain forests, lush padi fields, emerald lakes, white and black beaches, and clear, tranquil, turquoise lagoons.

Once out of Malaysian waters, we cruise through the Tarutao Marine National Park in the Butang group of islands in Southern Thailand. Just one beautiful sight after another. We'll pull baits the entire time we are cruising these waters, and it is here that we catch our first fish of the trip. The crew is extra hyped now that fish are on board. 'Aris seems to know what kind of fish it is, but the hell if I can understand the translation. I don't know the English name for the fish anyway. Note to self: buy a fish book at first opportunity.

We decide we'll anchor for the night further north, away from any kind of tourist development, in the middle of nowhere at Rok Nok. It's a marine national park, and according to the cruising guide, there are safe anchorages and supposedly amazing coral gardens. We are safely anchored well before sunset with brightly colored fish literally underneath the boat. I can't help myself; I'm overboard into the

water, drawn in by the beauty and the colors. I decide to do my first dive of the season, check all of my equipment and to teach the crew their responsibilities in this endeavor. A person could dive for hours here; it's not necessary to go very deep to encounter marine life of every possible color imaginable.

The crew washes up my dive gear and cooks their fish. I've learned that bathing on the swim platform underneath the evening sunset while sitting at sea level is celestial bliss. It certainly beats the small, tight shower inside the boat. When exiting from the sea with my swimsuit on, I might as well use the fresh water on the swim platform to lather up, wash my hair and shave amid nature. The crew knows to "disappear" when they see me materialize with my caddy of toiletries and large lush towel. However, no matter where you bathe on the boat, shaving the "bikini line" is not an easy task; it's absolutely necessary to take steps to resolve this quandary in the near future.

I open a bottle of the port wine and watch the spectacular jewel-toned sunset; soon I find myself lounging on the aft deck beneath the stars. It's a special feeling when you are out on the sea alone, staring at the full moon like a lover, all the time swaying to the rhythm of the universe and listening to the calls

of nature. I count every blessing that I have and give thanks. Amen.

The next morning, we are underway rather quickly, considering it's vacation time; we get to Ao Chalong and successfully check in before sunset, as the anchoring and shore entrance can be tricky. Now that we are in Phuket, and legally, I want to determine a good place to spend Christmas. I hear from the other yachtsman that the Boathouse at Kata Beach is a great place for that; they offer festivities on both Christmas Eve night and Christmas Day, and it's mostly the yachtsmen that are in attendance.

With my own yacht, I find that I'm inclined to revisit the same places that I coveted on the long-tail boat. The next morning, I make a loose plan and route for the next few days; we start our engines, our classical music and are underway. We eventually cruise to Kata Bay, where I take the dinghy ashore to the Boathouse to make some inquiries, and hopefully will make reservations for a Christmas dinner.

Once on shore, I know to pull the dinghy way up for when the tide comes in; the dinghy with the engine is very heavy, too heavy for me to pull alone. Plenty of beach guys come to my rescue immediately; we pull it up about forty feet to a definite safe

spot, and I tie it to the swim rope; a large, thick rope marking the safe area for swimmers where no watercraft may enter.

I find the Boathouse is a small beachfront boutique hotel featuring Thai décor with a tropical feel, housing the open-air Boathouse Wine & Grill that claims to be an award-winning restaurant, serving French cuisine with matching wines from their own cellar. I order a glass of wine and request the hostess come to my table to discuss the holiday festivities and options.

The table next to me is a large, diverse group, very lively and laughing loudly, enjoying life. Once the hostess and I finish our conversation, I make a reservation for Christmas Eve dinner. I can't help but to overhear some of the conversations taking place on the next table; it seems they are all "yachties," having just met and are sharing "dinghy" stories.

Shortly I'm invited to join them and have no hesitations in sharing some camaraderie with my "mates." After several more glasses of wine and many more "dinghy" stories, my sides are in stitches. I decide that while I still have my senses, I need to head back to *Lady Satrece,* so I can still manage the dinghy.

Satrece

As I am walking back to where the dinghy is safely secured, I can't help but laugh out loud recalling the stories that I had just heard. As I'm nearing the location where my dinghy should be, I see a dinghy that has been secured to the swim rope, but the tide has raised about twenty feet higher, pulling the nose of the dinghy into the water while the tail of it and the engine are nearly vertical in the air.

As I bellow with laughter, I say out loud, "Some poor inexperienced *fool* is in for a surprise…at least they'll have a great dinghy story to tell!" As my laughter continues, I walk by the distressed dinghy looking for my own. It's now dark, and nothing seems familiar; where's my dinghy? I walk further and then retrace my steps. *Has someone stolen my new dinghy?* I then see something high on shore I had used as a marker when I tied up the dinghy. I turn and look toward the sea. "Oh, shit!" That vertical dinghy, twenty feet out in the water, *is mine*! The tide had come in about sixty feet, I look skyward, and it's a full moon; a *freaking* moon tide!

I stand there staring in shock and distress, as others walk by laughing at the *fool* who did this to their dinghy. I can't radio the crew for help because

they're on *Lady Satrece* with no way to shore. It's up to me.

I drop my backpack on shore and enter the water up to my chest, then dive down in the dark sea and attempt to untie the secure line. It takes me several dives, but the dinghy is untied and level again. However it's more than half filled with water and hardly floating. Fortunately, the engine still looks unharmed. I wipe the seawater from my face only to see my hands covered in black; great, my mascara is streaked down my cheeks. I cup my hands together in efforts to scoop the water out from the dinghy. I scoop and scoop and scoop and scoop, but little progress is made. Maybe, just maybe, it is emptied enough that the dinghy can hold me with the remaining water, so I climb in. Down we go, dinghy and I! I jump out immediately, so it doesn't sink. Perplexed and discouraged, I gather myself again and start scooping with a vengeance. After thousands of scoops and several rests, I decide to test it again; I hop in, and it stays afloat!

I say a prayer that the gas tank, line and motor have maintained their integrity. I grip the handle connected to the rope, and firmly pull once, pull twice, and it starts! I yell to someone walking by on shore

to toss me my backpack and off I go, knowing this was a close one.

As 'Aris hears me and the dinghy approaching, as standard operating procedure, he greets me to take the dinghy line and shines a spotlight for me to make a safe entry. He immediately notices that I'm barely afloat and am sitting in a dinghy full of water. His eyes open wide, and his mouth falls open as I toss him the line. I crawl up and on board, brush past him without an explanation like nothing had happened. By the time that I'm out of sight, the Kap' joins him, and I hear an outburst of laughter. They spend the next few minutes in an animated conversation trying to guess what happened to the "Boss Lady."

The next morning as I exit my cabin, the din-ghy is in order like nothing had happened, nothing is mentioned either, but every time I look at either crew, it's all they can do to NOT laugh.

I have my French-pressed coffee, eat my instant noodle cup of soup for breakfast, and we are ready to pull anchor. It's only two days until Christmas Eve, so I don't want to go too far. We set our compass to Koh Yao Islands. Despite their proximity to Phuket, Koh Yao Noi and Koh Yao Yai are barely touched by the mass tourism. The islands are located in the

middle of the striking emerald green Phang Nga Bay with limestone monoliths dotting the horizon in place of towering buildings. The seaside paradise has no traffic or chain stores, just a few local eateries and vendors pedaling trinkets. It's a low-key locale with secluded golden sand beaches. I spend most of the next two days swimming, snorkeling, dinghy exploring, diving and feasting while sipping Mekong whisky with ginger ale and lime. Surely, this is what heaven is like, complete with kitties onboard!

Christmas Eve evening we are anchored back in Kata Bay, and I begin dressing for a special dinner out. It's the first time on the boat that I'm attempting to apply full makeup other than mascara and lip gloss, and I'm actually styling my hair instead of donning the easy ponytail. 'Aris will deliver me to shore; I am not going to allow another dinghy incident tonight. I will radio the boat when I am ready to return.

Attired in my nicest sundress with rhinestone sandals in hand, I step down into the dinghy, and we are underway. As 'Aris curves inward to shore around the swim rope, he picks up speed. I'm thinking just *how cool* life is, when suddenly, I'm thrown from the dinghy and sent sailing through the air. I land in Kata Bay about twenty feet from the dinghy, plunged deep

in the sea! As I surface, backpack on, rhinestone san-
dals in hand, all I can think about is how my hair and
makeup are *ruined*! *And what the hell happened?*

By the time I surface, 'Aris has already determined the cause of impact that sent me sailing, but
as he sees me surface with a scowl across my face,
makeup smeared everywhere, sandals still in hand,
bobbing in the water, he opens his mouth to tell me
what happened, and laughter bellows out. He quickly
turns his head from me to gather himself, but once
he tries to speak again, the laughter continues. After
an extended amount of time, I'm still bobbing in
the water waiting for an explanation, but he *still* can't
speak to me. I toss him my sandals and backpack,
kick up into the dinghy, and all he can manage to do
is point downward beside the motor. I see that the
five-inch swim rope had broken away from its buoy
and had caught in our propeller, propelling me out
of the boat. We turn around and slowly return to
Lady Satrece, the Kap' hears the dinghy approach and
meets us at the swim platform, only this time, the
Kap's eyes are open wide, and his mouth falls open.
Again, as I get out of sight heading toward my cabin,
I hear 'Aris tell the Kap' what has happened, and the
laughter ensues for days!

distraction

It's an uneventful dinner in my humbled state, simply dressed with no makeup on and my hair in a ponytail; however, it's still enjoyable. Merry Christmas.

We spend the next week retracing steps of awesome places that I had already visited such as Koh Phi Phi and Maya Bay, then northward to the emerald waters of Phang Nga Bay with the gravity-defying limestone formations jutting out of nowhere, creating a vibe of sailing into a sci-fi movie. From there, we head southeast spending the night at Koh Khai or Chicken Island. This island is unique in that it has a bizarre rock spire formation which resembles the head of a chicken. Then when the tide goes out, silky white sand surfaces are apparent that connect the three islands together. It has one of my favorite little huts serving delectable fresh squid and other seafood.

We find ourselves anchored at Ao Nang for New Year's Eve. I decide to make no plans for the evening, as I'm already happy as a clam. I allow the crew to go ashore for the evening to participate in the festivities, but they too choose to remain on *Lady Satrece* as we are anchored in a heavenly spot off the beach, framed by the huge limestone rock-face cliffs

at the southern end of the beach and a skyscraper-sized rock towering offshore at the other.

About two hours before midnight, we begin witnessing a most incredible sight: a unique Thai floating lantern festival in celebration of the New Year. Thousands and thousands of stunning floating lanterns are released into the sky until the stroke of midnight, gently floating away, just above our boat. The further and further the lanterns travel and the more they fill the sky, it looks as though a new constellation is forming overhead. We recline on the boat and observe firsthand this touching moment, stirring each of us, an occasion that I will never forget.

We relax on New Year's Day and determine our route for the last week of the trip. The next morning we're own our way to check out at Ao Chalong, and then we will head slowly southbound back toward Malaysia, visiting all the outer islands that we cruised by on our way here. I no longer fear getting in trouble with immigration, as I realize we only enter the islands for meals and spend the rest of the time exploring the waters in *Lady Satrece*.

The feature highlight on the return trip is a spot the other "yachties" insist we explore. We arrive at Koh Muk and carefully search for a well-hidden

crevice in the cliff face, chronicled to us in minute detail, similar to using a treasure map searching for the lost loot. We find the discreet spot and anchor, and I take my mask and snorkel to investigate the cave opening. Fortunately, we arrive at the perfect time; it's an ebb tide, so the tide is falling. The cave is now exposed by nearly eight inches, so I venture into the cave with my mask, snorkel, fins, and gloves rather than retrieving my full dive gear. With my underwater flashlight, I swim through the Koh Hong or sea cave, which is a winding, pitch-black sea tunnel. It's an eerie and ominous feeling but highly stimulating, and the tunnel is longer than I thought. I'm having my doubts, when I suddenly see the "light at the end of the tunnel" and emerge into a lost world! I surface on a small white beach entirely enclosed 360 degrees on an awe-inspiring oasis in the interior of this mountain or limestone formation. This lost lagoon is an old pirate hangout overgrown with trees and greenery with wild calls of monkeys and birds echoing through and through. I feel alive and exhilarated! Immediately, I am envisioning and contemplating camping here tonight and building a large campfire, but I eventually come to my senses and decide that I'd better exit the cave before the tide

rises, and I can't swim through it with the occasional use of my snorkel. *And* could there be snakes or bats inside here?!

We arrive back at Langkawi where *Lady Satrece* and the crew will stand by until my return in about five to six weeks, when we will embark on the second voyage of this season. I stay two nights getting everything situated and also recruiting Barbara from the neighboring sailboat to watch the kitties, which are now about four weeks old and adorable. As I'm departing, the crew tell me that they can't wait for my return as this has been the best time of their lives, and they have found Nirvana.

Upon my return in the third week of February, I find the crew raring to go and four bow-legged fat kittens running all over the boat. The kittens had spent their entire life on the boat, and as it rocked side to side with the waves, the kittens' legs adjusted with an exaggerated curvature, looking like an entirely new breed of animal.

We returned to Thailand and continued to explore more and more of the islands. At the end of the season, I fly home, while the crew along with two hired hands deliver *Lady Satrece* back to Indonesia.

distraction

We have just enough time to get her serviced and maintained to kick off the peak season here in our part of the world.

The cats innately recognize their home and their mother, and they immediately exit the boat for the first time since birth. To this day, you can see four bow-legged cats running, playing and living at the docks.

21

Returning Home after Leaving Prince Charming

I arrive in Semarang from Jakarta after departing from Ron; Rifan and David greet me at the airport and load my luggage into the four-wheel drive, and we begin the rest of the journey home.

"So, sis, how was your week?

"It was phenomenal."

"So you enjoyed yourself?"

"More than you can imagine."

"Yeah? That's fantastic. I told you that you should go. I hope you got a good break and some rest because there's *a lot* of work to do. I told the factory to absolutely, positively *not* call you for *anything*."

"Oh really, why did you do that? That explains a lot. What's going on? How was your week?"

Six weeks in Indonesia and a week in my factory, David's suddenly the expert and proceeds to tell *me* all about *my* factory, as if I didn't know. "Man, there's a lot of shit that happens on a daily basis. Do you know all the shit that goes on there? Did you know that 'stuff' is delivered there every day all day long—sandpaper, finishing products, all shapes and sizes of brass handles, knobs, hinges, foam, fabric, lighting, various shapes and sizes of glass panes, and even boxes of broken glass used for somethin'. The deliveries just never stop! Are you aware that the same people checking the stuff in and doin' the inventory, are probably the people that could figure out how to steal it too? I think we need to change your systems …" And he goes on and on. There are obviously a lot more systems in place that he knows of, but maybe some of them can be improved upon too. Gjeeshk! Sitting in the backseat alone, I disappear into my own little world, and my brother never stops talking. Blah, blah, blah, blah, blah is all I hear.

As I peer outside the car windows watching the masses, I see food carts and scooters, I see the shanties and slums, an ample amount of colorful

sarongs on the people and laundry drying, hanging on most anything. I see mothers walking with their babies, tossing them into the air or breastfeeding them. There are old men standing wrapped in their sarongs without a shirt, rubbing their tummies with one hand while stretching with the other. I see naked children playing in the filthy river water, others brushing their teeth in it while others bathe or use it for a toilet. I see plenty of oxen, cows, goats, and chickens. There's always the multitude of broken-down scooters and trucks parked on side of the road, many of them being worked on, and many of them abandoned.

Every time I'm on a journey home on these roads, in the midst of the masses, taking it all in and studying these sights, it takes a second look to see why I love living here. I see the lively and animated chatter going on at the food carts, that the shanties and slums are serviced with care, that the clothes are clean and pressed with pride, the mothers are feeling blessed to have their babies, the old men smiling because they know the younger family members are taking care of them. The children are having a blast swimming while others are feeling clean and fresh from their mandis. The animals tell the story that

there is enough food in this area. It never ceases to amaze me how these people maintain their dignity and self-respect while likewise preserving their happiness and smiles.

Taking a closer look *today*, I see the hardships and misery that have come to the people. Their faces mirror my heart. To see their suffering deepens the gloom, the emptiness, that I'm feeling.

"What's wrong with you, sis? You're awfully quiet today. Did something happen this week?" David asks defensively.

"No, nothing happened at all. Matter of fact, it was perfect."

"So, he was a good guy, huh?" David says openly in front of Rifan, knowing that Rifan hardly understands any English.

"Yes, he was."

"Will you see him again?"

"I don't know. I don't know how or when. It's like it's been the perfect week, and I was Cinderella. I can't help but wonder if I'd think as highly of him in the real world, outside of a five-star hotel and Wonderland."

"What are you talking about?"

"What would you think if I were to ask him here this weekend? I'd like to know if he was real, *it* was real or if we just lived out a fantasy."

"Sis, you can't do that! You have too much to lose! To have a man visit you at your home while living in the middle of the fundamental and fanatical Muslims? No way!"

With a long sigh, "Yeah, I know…you're right." My spirits are crushed.

At home that night after dinner, David is smoking a cigar and drinking Bintang. I am drinking a cocktail courtesy of the generous reserves Ron sent to Jepara. We are both sitting in silence, listening to the soft hypnotic music and the calls of the nature.

"Sis, are you sure you're okay? What's wrong? Tell me."

"I can't stop thinking about Ron…and the week we had. It was phenomenal…very special."

"You mean you actually care about this guy; he could be someone special to you?"

"Yes, I do…I *think* he could. I'd just like to know if something could really come of this; otherwise, he will return to America, and we'll both be left wondering and suffering until we know."

"How would you know?"

"I would like to see him in a different environment, like in real life. I wonder how he would fare here in my world, what he would think of me after seeing...all of this?" Satrece says as she waves her arms around at the compound and its contents.

"It'd blow the dude's mind, sis." David chuckles.

"I wish he could come *here*...this weekend, and then I would know, *we* would know."

"Well, sis, if you really feel that way, let's find out. Let's do it."

"You said it yourself, David, I can't do that. you were absolutely right," Satrece resigns herself.

"As *you* always say, if there's a will, there's a way."

I stare and study David, if he's on board, and with his help, maybe this *can* be done.

"C'mon, sis, you can figure this out. What do we have to do?"

"Firstly, I need to call Ron and see if he's interested and can swing it in his schedule. Hang on, I'll be right back."

"Ron's on board. He said he'd move mountains if needed, but he will be here. He's very concerned for my reputation and me, and rightfully so. Ron fully

understands the risks and consequences involving his visit."

For the next two hours, David and I conspire and scheme, and the full plan is devised. Now to put it into motion.

As Ningseh and Rifan enter the house the next morning, I gather them for a meeting. "I've just learned that we'll have a guest in town to visit the factory. Rifan, you'll pick him up from the airport on Friday evening…tomorrow evening, and we'll cook and serve dinner for him here at the house. I'll make you a sign for the airport. Sama sama, the same as we do for every customer/prospect that visits. Let's make sure the house and car are perfectly clean and in order today. Ningseh, we'll plan a dinner menu this evening when I return home from work. Let's get extra flowers from the flower market. Get birds of paradise, lilies, and the local sedap malams, so the fragrance floats through the house during the evening dinner. Buy any other brightly colored flowers that are there and lots of them. You two have worked extra hard with David visiting and have to work late Friday night, why don't you take off Saturday? Ningseh, if you'd please make a pot of your tradi-

338

tional Sumatran curry, chapattis and riata sauce for David and me on Saturday and bake a chicken for Sunday dinner…that will do us great. Then both of you can relax for a long weekend. Good plan…any questions? You know what to do. Terima Kasih!"

Upon entering the factory the next morning, the staff gets their needed time with me. Now it's my turn. "We are having a guest visit the factory. Mr. Roger can't make it, so he has sent his associate, Mr. Ron. He'll travel here Friday evening and will be here in the factory Saturday morning. Let's do the normal things we do for a customer visit. Clean the factory extra well Friday evening. I will evaluate our 'finished stock lists' and make a list for you to open up the pieces for display in the quality control room. Please see that we have refreshments; also that we have a catalogue, a disc, samples of wood colors, and fabric swatches. Biasa saja, just the normal things."

"Yes, Ms. Satrece," everyone complies.

"Oh, Susi, see if you can book the new bunga-low on the beach for our guest on Friday night."

Will I get away with this, or will I be ruined?

22

Can He Make the Cut?

*F*riday evening. "I've landed and am in good hands," Ron gushes.

"Welcome to Central Java. How has everything gone so far?" I ask.

"Great, no problems. I saw your driver with his sign as soon as I exited the plane; the SUV was parked in front of the terminal, and we're on our way. I see you've made me a playlist for the ride to your home, and I received a goody bag with beer, water, fruit and nuts. And what's this? A cute letter telling me I have about three hours plus…so sit back and relax. 'Rifan' is your driver's name. You've covered it all."

"Well, it's nothing like the welcome you had for me in Jakarta, but we do our best."

distraction

"I can't wait to see you, I'm so excited," Ron says in a husky voice.

"I'm very excited too."

"I can't wait to see your home, your factory and to meet your brother."

"Uh, yeah…that's all going to be…very interesting."

Nearly four hours later, "Sis, sit down, you're making me a nervous wreck. Are you that excited? Sit down!"

At nearly the same moment, Rifan calls at the designated time, "Ms., we've just passed the factory, so we'll be home in less than twenty minutes. Ada macat banyak …the traffic has been heavy."

"Hebat! Great! How's the guest doing?"

"Not so good, he's getting very impatient. He keeps asking me how much further, how much further?"

Little does Rifan know that Ron can understand everything he is telling me in Bahasa. I hear a big laugh in the background as Ron hears us talking about him.

Rifan nears our front gate and gives a honk, my sign that they've arrived and for Bidjo to open the security gate. Ron bounds out of the SUV and

is already at the front door before Rifan gets parked; Rifan's not moving fast enough for him. The door is unlocked for Ron, and he pushes through long before I can get there to greet him. He enters the office/gym/library room and sees the opposite door to the pavilion area. Ron is quickly through this door, nearly running into me, and a little disoriented. Most people aren't used to entering a house and going through the next door into the outside again, the open pavilion area. Ron pauses, taking in the night, the music, the fountains, the birds, the candles and torches, incense and everything else. All I see is a great big smile and teeth; I would say that Ron is a happy man to be here. He grabs me in a bear hug, picking me up off the floor, just like the normal greeting from every other customer that comes through. Ron isn't playing his part too well!

David says, "By the size of the smiles on your faces, I'm not goin' to be welcome here for long."

Ron places me on my feet on the floor, and I make the introductions. Ron hands David a fifth of Jack Daniels and a box of Cuban cigars. "Oh, WOW, man! A man after my own heart. Thank you, thank you very much, man!"

That's it; Ron has won David over in the first two minutes of being in the house. Ron thanks David for helping create and execute our charade to allow him to visit. I have African music blaring through the house, the drum beats adding to the electrifying charge already permeating the night air. David and Ron have a seat as I fix Ron a cocktail and instruct Ningseh and Rifan on the final timeline for serving dinner. Sascha wastes no time jumping up on the coffee table working her way toward Ron; she sits and studies him. She greets him with a few "meows," introducing herself. Ron can't help but notice her and glances down, then leans forward and scratches Sascha's ear. *Wah lah, another friend is made. In ten minutes, Ron has won over my two significants; why couldn't it be that easy for me to trust him?*

Ningseh and Rifan serve us a beautiful meal of grilled salmon and dill sauce, couscous with pine nuts and parsley accompanied by spinach gnocchi. We eat homemade pineapple upside-down cake for dessert, while all the time the African drums continue their electrifying beats. I sit in my normal seat at the head of the table with Ron to my left and David to my right. I notice how much Ron is enjoying himself,

and how he is as comfortable with David as he had been with me.

Once dinner is finished, I need to implement the next step of our plan. I tell Ningseh and Rifan that David is here, so he'll chaperone the guest while here in my home, and that David has offered to take the guest to the hotel later tonight. They are thrilled to be excused earlier than expected; they can go home now. "Enjoy your extra day off tomorrow, thank you for all of your hard work." Plan executed. Staff gone. We're free!

I guess David misses civilization more than he knows; he visits until the wee hours of the morning. He forgets *his* next part of the plan—*leave*! That is, go to the hotel, his cute bungalow on the beach. Too many whiskeys later, we decide that he should crash in his room here and move to the beach tomorrow.

Ron and I retire to my room illuminated by candles of all shapes and sizes on every surface. Aromatherapy fills the air, allowing rose and lavender scents to bombard our senses. I have desire on my mind, so the negligee I select is frilly with a delicate satin and lace lining, the reveal of it is a sweet tease. Ron's eyes move across my breasts to the peekaboo lace delicately cupping my breasts. Like a

stately prince, Ron sweeps away his shirt and shoes and unbuttons the top of his jeans.

We lay across my bed, but Ron is still very charged and excited, thrilled to be here, fascinated by my home and can't stop chatting about his experiences of the day. Sascha hops up on the bed, chooses a spot just above our heads and curls up. Ron naturally reaches up to stroke her; she gives him a soft meow saying, "I like you too."

"Sascha …" Ron addresses my sweet little Persian kitty, "I need a little privacy with your mom. Do you mind?"

And with a perfect understanding, as if English were Sascha's first tongue, she meows softly and jumps off the master bed. She curls up in her own carpeted spiral penthouse at the other end of the palatial room.

"Darling, are you okay with David being so close by in his room tonight?" With genuine concern, Ron questions me.

"It's okay, I'm sure he is as good as passed out by now; I just really don't care." I arch a threatening brow.

Ron replies with a sardonic and sexual smile. "Neither do I."

At once, we are holding on to one another as if violins are playing right outside in the night air. My whole body becomes one pleasure vessel only to be satisfied by Ron. He can hardly contain his desire for me. He slides his hand down to the hem of my royal purple satin babydoll nightgown, his eyes hold mine, and as if answering the bid of Aladdin, I sit up, and Ron pulls my gown up and over my head, leaving me only in my panties. I place my hand on his chest and feel every sinew; I want to draw my name in the thick mane of hair that covers his chest.

All the evening's teasing and tormenting was just too maddening for us. With one move, his motion is smooth, and his mission is clear to me; he drives himself into me which is all I wanted from the instant I laid eyes on him today. His thrusts are brutal, heavenly and strong, as he too is overcome with denied passion. My aching self is filled, and my tight nipples are throbbing. As if electricity is driving my hips, they buck and lift Ron, feeling him fill me, pinning me beneath him.

I rise up, cry out in relief, and I feel him come with a final driving push. I gasp while lying back beneath the pleasure-filled moans of Ron's roaring

climax. There is no intrusion, no disturbance from outside our sweet room of pleasure.

I lie against his chest. He cradles me, rocks me, he never stops kissing me. He covers me with long, desirous kisses that continue to cook my postcoital rapture. And when I suck his nipples and bite at them playfully, he is hard again and pushing against me.

It was not until a third time that we laid still. I turn into his arms, and together, we spoon until we fall into our own peaceful slumber. I feel I have found a piece of heaven, and I never want to awaken from such a perfect and peaceful place.

We sleep in a little late. I call the factory and say I'm waiting on the guest, and as soon as he is delivered to my home, I'll bring him in. It's amazing how quickly I learn to lie. Ron sees me for the first time in my normal attire: khaki clothes, hiking boots, ponytail and little makeup. He seems to be okay with it. I drive us to the factory. Ron isn't used to being driven by a woman. He can't stop laughing at it all: the normal detours, the small one-lane roads filled with five lanes of people, ox carts, bikes, scooters, buses, cars and trucks, etc. He ducks and jerks a few times; he's making me nervous and I miss several

gears. Ron laughs more and more, which adds to my nervousness.

We arrive at the factory. In the office, I introduce Mr. Ron to the staff: Huda, Susi, and Sofie. He surprises them by speaking Bahasa. Mr. Ron still isn't playing his part too well; he's supposed to be a furniture dude here straight from America, not an oil and gas dude having lived in Jakarta, knowing the language and local customs. Mr. Ron quickly charms them all and has them engaged and laughing.

I begin the tour of the factory in the quality control room where some of my finest pieces are displayed for Mr. Ron. He is taken aback, the first serious look I've seen on his face since his arrival. Ron is utterly fascinated, and I can see his brain spinning, wondering if he could have done this. Could he have created this factory or these exquisite furniture designs? Ron keeps reaching for my hand, and I keep pushing it away. "Remember your part," I chide. I take Mr. Ron through the rest of the factory; we continue into the sanding room and follow the process a piece of furniture would go through. I introduce him to the department heads, and he responds in Bahasa, engaging them all. Ron is already treating each person like they will soon be his distant relative.

Ron can't conceive the complexity of the factory, yet its simplicity. At the end of the tour, I escort Ron to the office and into the conference room, as I normally would any other client. Behind the closed doors (yet big windows) is the time to discuss production schedules and pricing. Ron spends this time questioning me how I manage my cost basis and profit centers. I jump at the opportunity to present my systems, to have another bright mind to review my processes. Can it be improved? I *always* worry about this with the fluctuating currency and the vast number of materials used. After an in-depth investigation, I receive kudos, and am relieved.

I inform the staff that we are wrapping up the visit, and I'm taking Mr. Ron back to his hotel, and tell them good-bye for the weekend. I take Ron on the big Jepara tour. We go to the beach first, a beautiful place on the Java Sea with turquoise waters and white sand. We don't stay long, for the same reasons I hesitate visiting as often as I would like; it's very hot and too many men drinking too much Bintang Beer. We drive along the coast where possible and conclude our tour at a place I call the French Village, a new compound on the sea, built entirely of local style prefab bungalows. It seems the French people

have populated most of the place quickly; hence, the name. It has a small swimming pool and a Thai restaurant; it's a charming little place. Boy, has Jepara come a long way, baby! I order us a small Thai feast for our late lunch, as we sit with the sea breeze blowing in our faces. Several hours pass, Ron is full of questions; he wants to know everything about the factory, Jepara, the people and life here.

We return to my home in the late evening, and then shower to wash off the red Java clay and the light shimmer of sweat.

I sneak into the bedroom and light the aromatherapy and the full array of candles while Ron makes us martinis. We lounge underneath the vibrant stars and in front of the fountains and the lush, colorful tropical flora. The kitties are playing, and the birds are chirping. Life is perfect!

I ultimately take Ron's hand, and his eyes turn to seize mine as if a camera has captured this moment, catching the sensual connection that runs from my desire to his groin. In an understanding silence, he follows me into my bedroom. Catching the door behind us, Ron closes it gently; and with the click of the latch, electricity ignites within me more than ever. I turn to him and thrust myself into his arms.

distraction

He is pleasantly taken aback. Ron's mouth opens to devour my kisses ravenously. "You are my dream come true. You are my beauty, you are my prize." His lips feed upon my throat and my face. His manhood pushes against my tender belly.

With the burning candles surrounding the room, Ron's body seems like a polished piece of granite in the dim light. His hair is thick and lustrous. I throw my arms around his neck. His hands unzip my dress, and it falls to the floor; he releases me from my lace-filled bra and panties. I return the favor quickly, stripping him, and we stand nude, facing one another in a state of ravenous sensual desire.

I look up into his beautiful deep brown eyes and rise up on my tippy toes to mount him like a gentleman's stallion, climbing up to ride him in the most sensual way. I change my mind, and I push him backward, so he falls onto my bed. He grabs my hand, and I fall lightly on top of him.

I slide myself onto him; I can feel him seal himself against me. Slowly he sinks back onto my bed spread with navy and gold satin coverings that stretch out onto the pile of pillows that lie about. I throw my head back as I ride him, tall and very much in control.

Ron's hands lift my breasts as I straddle him. He pinches my nipples and holds them throbbing as I buck and rear upon his shaft, sliding up as high as I can without releasing my hold and plummeting down; my lips pucker and dip to kiss this delicious man of mine.

Ron's face darkens with his groans and as I feel his organ erupt under me. I come, bucking still, until I am transfixed; my legs outstretched and shimmering with the last shocks of our pleasure. We lie together in silence.

We are arm in arm, and slowly, Ron wipes my hair back from my face, whispering, "My darling Satrece," as he covers me with delicate kisses. My hips dip to kiss him back.

Quiet moments pass, and he starts to kiss me again. I close my eyes and flex my hips, enjoying his tender lips. Facing one another, attraction drives desire yet again. My hands slide down his legs, reaching for his manhood. He arches his hips, lifting them to meet my hungering hands.

He looks dark and alluring; his face filled with gracious pleasure. Ron whispers to me, "I'm ready for you, my darling." My eyes meet his gaze, and reaching in between his thighs, I grasp him firmly,

distraction

squeezing hard, my thumb brushes over the tip. "Aaahhh ..." Ron gasps.

"Darling ..."

I know he wants to come, but I want to culminate this sexual encounter with the perfection we both want, the perfection we both deserve. I push hard and fast onto him. "Aaaahhhh...baby, you're so warm and wet," Ron cries out. He is buried inside me, filled with elation. Breath escapes from his body as my eyes close, and pleasure erupts from the back of my throat.

We cry out together as our bodies take over in sync as if playing in a harmonious symphony.

"My darling Satrece, oh my darling!"

"Ron, my dear stallion!"

I hold him, and he holds me. We are willing and lustful of each other. We find ourselves wanting to physically possess each other.

Throwing my head back, as my hair tumbles around and down my back, we begin to ignite. He grabs my hips, holding me as we shout incoherently through our orgasm. I tighten my hold in his hands, and silently, we lose ourselves as we explode together, his organ inside of mine.

We climax, folding over into one another as our bodies writhe with passion in the most glorious way. We are complete, together now. We began as two hot bodies desiring the other, but now we lie together as one.

We awake Sunday morning. I feel exhilarated, fulfilled, and complete. I wonder if Ron is feeling the same. I remember his passion during our lovemaking last night, and I know by the look on his face that he is.

After such a wonderful evening, I truly desire that first precious cup of "java." I French press us a pot of "kopi" and demonstrate to Ron how fragrant and oily these local Indonesian coffee beans are. "These beans are magnificent. Maybe the nicest you will ever smell and taste," I say as I run my fingers through them.

"Mmm…I can't wait to indulge in this *coffee*, I also see it's made with extra TLC," Ron says.

I carry a tray back to the bedroom, we crawl into bed, lean back onto our posh pillows and indulge in our coffee; our legs are thrown across one another, and we engage in conversation for our millionth hour.

"I'm not sure what we do today in Jepara, Ron, you've seen it all."

"What would you normally do?"

"I would sometimes go to the beach. Otherwise, I would treadmill, meditate, read, play with the kitties or, if I'm lucky, catch a movie on television. Sunday is my only day off, so I keep it low key."

"Well, I know what I would like to do today."

"What's that?"

Ron takes my coffee cup out of my hand and sets it aside. He leans over me, looks me in the eyes and proceeds to kiss me slowly and then ravenously. He wraps his arms around me and entangles his legs in mine. *Ahhhh! I know what he wants to do today.* We act like bunnies, and we make love time and time again.

Come late afternoon, I say, "I know what we can do now. I bought several seasons of *Boston Legal* when I was in the States. Are you familiar with that series? In my limited knowledge of television, it's my favorite."

"Yes, of course I'm familiar with *Boston Legal*, it's *my favorite* too!"

"Really, unbelievable! I'm now watching season five, which is probably reruns for you."

"I travel so much, I've missed more than I've seen. That's fine."

I fix us a late lunch from the food Ningseh has prepared. We take our teak trays into the bedroom and watch *Boston Legal* for the next several hours. We laugh and laugh. I love this series, but today, it's funnier than ever, and the chicken and vegetable curry also is tastier than ever.

We bathe and freshen up. Then we make ourselves a martini. The *"real"* last night for us. Ron departs Monday morning at 6:30 a.m., after Bidjo leaves but before Ningseh and Rifan arrive. I've hired a contract car and driver to deliver Ron to the Semarang airport, where he will travel to Singapore for one last meeting before departing to the U.S.

We enjoy another evening and a late night of gentle kisses filled with sweet, passionate lovemaking. At last I say, "Darling, you should probably get some rest; there's an early morning wake-up call for you, and you have an important meeting tomorrow."

"I don't want to sleep. I want to spend every minute I can with you, my love. There will be plenty of time to sleep when we are apart."

We finally doze off in each other's arms in the wee hours of the morning. The alarm buzzes. Ron

reaches over, softly strokes my cheek and gently kisses me as to not wake me. "Good morning, my angel," he whispers.

I allow him to think that I'm barely awake and am quickly back to sleep. He is up and in the shower, and I just lie in bed and hug my pillows. It seems that I've been stripped of all my will, all my strength, and my power to be. I can't move or my world will crash. So much for the hearty breakfast I promised.

Ron reenters the bedroom wrapped in a towel and walks over to me; I continue to pretend to be sleeping, so he begins packing his suitcase. I watch his every deliberate move; it's obvious he has packed a million times before. He looks around at me, I quickly close my eyes again, and he gives me a loving smile. He has something on his mind; he wants to tell me something, but I don't want to hear it. *What's wrong with me?* I should be assisting him, I should be talking to him, I should be doing something, anything but pretending that I'm asleep. Ron dresses. He feels me watching him, he turns around again, and I just stare back, listless and speechless.

"My precious, you're awake."

"I've been awake, I've been watching you. Sorry I didn't make you breakfast; my legs just don't seem to want to move."

"That's okay, I couldn't eat anything anyway."

Ron comes back to bed fully dressed, curls up around me and holds me. Our hearts beat in rhythm together; our souls serenade each other, but our lips remain in silence. What is there to say?

I receive a phone call from the driver; he and the car have just arrived. Like moving in slow motion, we get up, grab Ron's bags and proceed to the front door. He's displaying the same strength I requested of him during our departure in Jakarta, but I, on the other hand, feel like a limp, breathless doll. We stop at the front door; he takes my face in both of his hands and kisses me lovingly.

"Satrece, I love you. I love you more than you'll ever know. Thank you for inviting me to your home this weekend. I knew when we met that you were a very special woman, and you have a very special life here. Thank you for sharing it with me."

I say nothing, I can't, and I just blink back tears. Ron senses I am struggling, so he graciously accepts my silence.

"I'll call you when I get to Singapore. I hope you have a good day, my love."

"Have a safe trip. Thank you for…for every-thing…for being you. Bye," I finally squeeze out.

With that, he's out the door, and the door closes between us. He's gone. I lean back on the door, look upward to God, waiting, I need something; comfort, answers, something. The answer is: my life will never be the same again. I have been the master of my own destiny, but now destiny has taken my power away. I *loved* my life, but now I see my life is without love, the romantic kind of love. *Today* is the day that the music died, the day the sun stopped shining, and the day the birds stopped singing.

While in the shower, I break into tears. I hav-en't felt pain like this since I learned my daddy was terminally ill. My heart aches fervently, I can hardly breathe, my stomach is in knots, and my entire body seems to be aching. There are tears rolling down my cheeks as I sob uncontrollably. God have mercy on me! Please have mercy!

I crawl back into bed only to find myself curled in a fetal position. Sascha curls up to me for support; she knows something is terribly wrong. "Sascha, I

found my soul mate, but he has gone." There is only distance between us now, and soon, we will be worlds away from one another.

Ningseh and Rifan enter; I inform them that I'll go into work late today.

"Ms., sakit?" (are you sick?) asks Rifan.

There is no hiding my red and puffy eyes. "Yes, I'm not feeling well today. I'm going to rest in my room longer before I go in." I call the factory and tell them the same. I can't enter the factory and allow everyone to see their fierce leader like this. You can't lead when your power is depleted; you can't create with no vision in sight or with tears rolling down your cheeks.

I have read that "'Tis better to have loved and lost than to never have loved at all." Well, that's bullshit! My world was *grand*! I'd been lucky in life, only unlucky in love, but who needed love anyway? Maybe I do…now? Damn him! Why did he do this to me? What can ever come of this? I grab my pillow, and with each hand holding a corner, I raise it over my head and slam it down on my bed, again and again. "Damn him! Damn him! Damn him!" I drop my pillow to the floor. I kick it with my right leg. I kick it with my left. Still kicking, throwing a full-fledged fit,

distraction

I shout, "Why did he do this to me? Why?!" I was fine. I didn't need *anyone*." He has left me in his wake, feeling broken. I've been brought down to my knees; the wings of love are crushed. "I wish he was here to hold me, to put his arms around me. Damn it! What in the hell am I saying? You big cry baby! I don't need a damn shoulder to lean on!" I scream into my pillow. My pillows have never known such abuse. Sascha huddles close by watching me, half hidden under the bed; she's not going to leave me alone, but she's never seen me like this before.

I tell Ningseh and Rifan that I'm still not feeling too well; I'll go in after lunch. I call the factory and tell them the same. Not only do I have red and puffy eyes, but swollen ones now.

Then "love" echoes through my mind. What? "Love." Did I fall in love with him? Is that what the problem is? Something caressed my soul, something touched me deep inside. "Don't be afraid of it. This is a gift from the universe. Embrace it," answers from above. Huh?

Ron calls. "How are you doing, my darling?" Ron asks softly.

"I've been better."

"Me too."

"So you're in Singapore?"

"Yes. I have the last meeting in a few hours, and then the flight back to the States later tonight. I have never dreaded going home so much in my entire life. It no longer feels like home."

"I can understand that."

"How's work today, darling?"

"I don't know, I haven't made it there yet?"

"Why's that? Is everything okay?" I could hear the concern in Ron's voice.

"Well…these stupid things called tears got in the way. Then I had a fight with my pillows. I can't let the people at the factory see me this way. I need for them to see strength and leadership, not my tears and weakness. Then these foolish thoughts and echoes are clouding my brain. Mercy, mercy!"

Ron laughs softly through my entire explanation. "I agree, you can't let them see you like this, but you cried tears for me?"

"Yes."

"Do you miss me?"

"Yes."

"I miss you so badly, Satrece. I've only just stopped crying myself. I forced myself to stop, so I could call you."

"Ron, what's next?"

"I don't know, my darling. We take it one step at a time. I've just found you; I'm not going to let you go. I've been looking for you my whole life."

"Ron, I love you." There I said it! The cat's out of the bag now.

"You love me?!" Ron asks incredulously. *Has she finally said it?*

"Yes, I love you."

"Oh, baby, I love you too!"

I feel much better after hanging up from Ron. I'm not going into work today, I decide. After all, how often do you fall in love? I want to luxuriate in it and savor it. The gift of love. I don't know what's next, but I'm not going to let *this gift* get buried by fear; I'm not going to hold out or hold back. I'm not going to give up or give in. Think, Satrece, think. What's next? Where there's a will, there's a way.

But who am I kidding? I just don't see any way forward, there isn't one. I'm immersed in commitments here with the villagers, the business, and my customers. I also have *Lady Satrece* and its crew on standby and am building my home in Bali. I have a fascinating, incredible and fulfilling life here, and I've spent fifteen years building it. How in the world can

this possibly work? How do I find room for a love-filled distraction? It's simply impossible, and my tears begin again.

The End

... or is it?

Top of the World

The Carpenters

Such a feeling's coming over me
There is wonder in most everything I see
Not a cloud in the sky, got the sun in my eyes
And I won't be surprised if it's a dream

Everything I want the world to be
Is now coming true especially for me
And the reason is clear, it's because you are here
You're the nearest thing to heaven that I've seen

About the Author

 Satrece grew up in a small town near Houston, Texas, and earned two engineering degrees from the University of Houston. Despite a personal tragedy in her life, she embraced her destiny and moved to Bali, Indonesia. With recovery and healing, she created a new life for herself. She began living the full adventure in Java by being an entrepreneur, a humanitarian, and a yachtsman exploring the waters of Southeast Asia in her spare time. Her first book, *distraction* launches a trilogy that will include the forthcoming *destiny* and *dubai.* She describes extraordinary years spent among exotic backdrops, where colorful details emerge from having lived the remarkable events herself.